The Civil Code of the Republic of China

Translator Chin-lin Hsia

Alpha Editions

This edition published in 2020

ISBN : 9789390382057 (Hardback)
ISBN : 9789390382972 (Paperback)

Design and Setting By
Alpha Editions
www.alphaedis.com
email - alphaedis@gmail.com

As per information held with us this book is in Public Domain.
This book is a reproduction of an important historical work. Alpha Editions
uses the best technology to reproduce historical work in the same manner
it was first published to preserve its original nature. Any marks or number
seen are left intentionally to preserve its true form.

THE CIVIL CODE

OF THE

REPUBLIC OF CHINA

Book I . . *General Principles*

Book II . . . . *Obligations*

Book III . *Rights over Things*

TRANSLATED INTO ENGLISH

by

CHING-LIN HSIA, M.A., B.SC., PH.D. (Edin.)
Member of Shanghai Bar Association
JAMES L. E. CHOW, B.A. (Cantab.)
Member of Shanghai Bar Association
Barrister-at-Law.
YUKON CHANG, B.SC.

Preface by	*Introduction by*
His Excellency HU HAN-MIN	Hon. FOO PING-SHEUNG
Member of the National	Chairman of the Foreign
Government of the Republic	Relations Committee of the
of China	Legislative Yuan
President of the Legislative	Chairman of the Civil Codi-
Yuan	fication Commission

SHANGHAI :
KELLY & WALSH, LIMITED
Hong Kong : : : Singapore
1930

Preface

Of all the works undertaken by the Legislative Yuan since the definite formation of the National Government in October 1928, the Civil Code, Books I, II and III of which are translated in the present volume, is by far the most important and the one which will have the greatest influence on the future of China.

The development of business relations beween Chinese and foreigners during the XIXth century, the introduction in our country of new ideas and new needs, the contact of the Eastern and Western civilizations, are raising every day juridical questions which the old imperial legislations as recorded in the Ta Tsing Lu Li are unable to solve.

Neither do these old legislations tally with the Three Principles (racial, democratic and social) of the late Dr. Sun Yat Sen, the fundamental basis of the political doctrine of the Kuomintang, on the application of which we hope to raise the material and intellectual conditions of the toiling masses of China, to usher the country into a new era of prosperity, and to secure to China in the great family of nations the position to which she is entitled by her area, her population and her millenary culture.

The new Civil Code follows in its theoretical portions the principles which the modern juridical science is spreading steadily all over the world and which are tending to constitute a sort of universal common law and to remove the discrepancies due to the dissimilarity of the various national legislations, thus facilitating the development of international relations. In this respect, its coming into force will strengthen the ties which link us with the friendly nations of the world and will foster our trade relations with them.

On the other hand, in order to meet the geographical, economic and demographic needs of a country with so many diversified regions as China, a number of old customs must be maintained in the present Code, principally in the matter of real rights. Many of its characteristics are therefore essentially Chinese.

Preface—continued

Finally, by embodying in it the principles of the Kuomintang the Code is given a decidedly social turn. The personal activity of the citizen is directed by the Code so that it may be most advantageous for the community to which the individual belongs. This particular feature distinguishes the new Code from the individualistic legislations of Europe and America as well as from the former Chinese legislation of the old familial type.

Viewed from these different aspects, it seems to us that the English translation of Books I, II and III of the Code by Dr. C. L. Hsia, Messrs. J. L. E. Chow and Yukon Chang may render great services not only to the sinologues who are making a special study of the Chinese law or to the students of comparative legislation, but to all who are interested in the problems of the Pacific and in the future of the Chinese Nation.

HU HAN-MIN.

NANKING, 1ST JUNE, 1930.

Foreword

The Drafting Committee of the Chinese Civil Code has decided not to issue any official translation of the Code. The Chinese text only is to hold good. Nevertheless, an English translation would serve the most useful purposes, not only to the student of comparative law, but to foreigners residing in our territory, now that their study and knowledge of our language have not yet sufficiently developed. We have therefore given every encouragement to Dr. Ching-Lin Hsia, Mr. James L. E. Chow and Mr. Yukon Chang in their translation of Books I, II and III and the laws of their application.

To render into a European tongue any Chinese literary text is not an easy task. The difficulty can be imagined when legislative documents are to be translated. The minutest shades here must be accurately reproduced if the true scope of the original provisions is to be preserved. Furthermore, a number of our expressions have had centuries of usage and correspond to customs and judicial conceptions which are peculiar to our country and have no exact equivalent in any foreign language.

Notwithstanding all these difficulties and the inevitable shortcomings of their enterprise, the authors had, however, all the advantages available. They have followed closely the discussions of the Drafting Committee as well as the proceedings of the meetings of the Legislative Yuan during which the draft was thoroughly examined and amended; they are fully acquainted with the meaning and scope of each article. We feel therefore that their translation gives the best English version of the Chinese text, and we do not hesitate to recommend it as such to the public.

FOO PING-SHEUNG, (*Chairman*)
CHAO YEH-TANG
SZE SHANG-QUAN
LIN PING
SOUMI CHENG
Members of the Drafting Committee of the Civil Code.

Introduction

I.

Codification is no new thing in China. Ever since the earlier periods of its development, the Chinese Empire was provided with books of rites such as the Chow-Li in which ethical rules could be found governing the relations of individuals to family and to government. These compilations took a more definite and more comprehensive form under the Tang dynasty when, in the year 654, the first real Chinese code was enacted. The Tang Code is the foundation on which Chinese legislation was built from the VIIth till the beginning of the XXth century. Its distribution and even part of its provisions were adopted by the Sung, Yuan and Ming Emperors, and the Manchus re-edited it in 1646 under the title of Ta-Tsing Lu-Li. The Ta-Tsing Lu-li was several times revised under the Manchu Emperors. Its 1799 edition (4th year of Kia King) was summarily translated into English by Sir George Staunton (1810) and into French (1812) by Renouard de Sainte-Croix, and Italian version was also published at the same date. The 1890 edition has been accurately and extensively rendered into French, with commentaries, notes and appendixes, by Father Gui Boulais (Shanghai, 1923-24).

The last revision was made only a short time before the fall of the Manchu dynasty. It is dated the year 1910 and was issued as the *Ta Ts'ing Hien-hing hing-lu*. It had not been abrogated or modified by the laws of Republican China, until the promulgation of the present code; and it still formed the foundation of the civil law which was in force all through the country at the time of the publication of the new civil code whose three first books are now presented to the public in the English version by Dr. C. L. Hsia, Mr. J. L. E. Chow and Mr. Yukon Chang.

The Ta-Tsing Lu-li covers the whole field of such parts of private and public law as the Chinese legal mind would

Introduction

then consider as reducible to written statutory provisions. It deals with administration, finances, army, public works, penal law, family law; few of its provisions relate to the law of obligations, which was left to be governed by custom. It is quite characteristic of the old traditional conception of Chinese civil law that it is not so much to regulate private intercourse between individuals and to delimit their respective rights than to preserve the general harmony of the universe. More emphasis is laid in the Ta-Tsing Lu-li on the duties of the people based on ethical principles, than on their claims. Every violation of a legal rule, although it might injure only a private interest and involve no criminal responsibility in the modern sense of the word, constitutes in this system a breach of the order of the world, the safeguard of which has been entrusted by Heaven to the Emperor, and therefore involves for its author not only civil consequences such as compensation for the damage caused, but a penalty for transgression of an ethical precept.

II.

However interesting this general conception of natural law might have been, it was no longer in keeping with the new activities and institutions that had been introduced into China based on the principles of western law, nor was it in keeping with the development of modern thought in intellectual Chinese circles. Whilst the jurists of the old classical school were compiling the last edition of the Ta-Tsing Lu-li, the movement for constitutional and legal reform had already started in Peking.

During the 28th year of the reign of Kuang Hsu, high Chinese officials had submitted to the Throne a memorandum suggesting that China should fundamentally transform her law, in order to keep pace with the progress of foreign nations. On the 25th day of the 3rd month of the 29th year of Kuang-Hsu (1904), the following edict was issued to Prince Tsa Tchen:

"The development of commercial relations, the encouragement to industry have always been the primary duty of the Government, and must be carefully attended to.

Introduction

We hereby order that Tsai Tchen, Yuan Shih Kai and Wu Ting Fang be commissioned to compile first a commercial code which will constitute the rule to be observed in commercial transactions."

A few months later, the three Commissioners submitted to the Emperor a draft law on Traders in nine articles, and a draft law on Commercial Companies in 131 articles. This was the beginning of the modern Chinese codification. The first Codification Commission (修訂法律館) was constituted two years later. In 1907, Chen Kia Pen (沈家本), Yu Lien San (俞廉三) and Ying Juan (英瑞) were appointed directors of the Commission, the staff being composed of returned law students from Japan, Europe and America, with a foreign adviser, Mr. Y. M. Matsuoka (松岡義正). The work of compiling a Civil Code was immediately started.

Since the new Code was to be a complete departure from the general structure and principles of the traditional Chinese law, it could not follow the distribution nor the phraseology of the Ta-Tsing Lu-li. Much had therefore to be imported from foreign jurisprudence, and the country from which the Codification Commission made their main borrowing was Japan. The reasons for this were obvious. Japan has just emerged from her old feudalism into a modern State. Her signal success in the process of modernization China was anxious to follow. It was quite natural for China to try to profit by her neighbour's experience. Besides, since the reform movement had been on foot in China, hundreds of Chinese in search of modern knowledge had gone to Japanese universities, principally to the Japanese law schools, where their studies were facilitated by the great similarity of the two languages. Japan at the time had completed her civil and commercial codification, which she had modelled principally after the German Codes.* She had created a technical legal Japanese vocabulary, translated a number of the leading

---

*The German Civil Code passed through three successive stages. Its first draft was submitted to the Chancellor of the German Empire on December 27th, 1887 and published in 1888. It was revised by a commission appointed in 1890, whose labours resulted in the establishment of a second draft, presented to the Reichstag on January 27th, 1896. The definitive text was promulgated on August 18th, 1896.

The Japanese Civil Code was drafted during the years 1893 to 1895 and promulgated on April 27th, 1896. Its compilers could scarcely have used the second German draft.

Introduction

juridical text books of Europe, and produced a large Japanese legal literature. The Chinese could then find in Japan an adaptation to the Far Eastern mind, in a language closely related to their own, of what represented at the time the most advanced stage of western scientific juridical science.

The outcome of the labours of the Codification Commission was a Draft Civil Code in five Books dealing respectively with General Principles, Obligations, Real Rights, Family and Inheritance. Books I, II and III including 1,316 articles were printed in 1911, the publication being dated the 5th day of the 9th moon of the 3rd Year of Huan Tung. Another 253 articles forming Books IV and V were completed and published later on. The whole work was entitled *Draft Civil Code of the Tsing Dynasty* (大清民律草案) and followed very closely the lines of the Japanese and German Codes.

After the proclamation of the Republic, and the abdication of the last Manchu Emperor (December, 1911—February 1912), the Draft was re-examined and was found inadequate in several respects. A Committee for the Compilation of Codes (法典編纂會) was formed and entrusted with the duty of preparing a new Draft. In 1916 the Committee was reorganized under the Presidency of Dr. Wang Chung Hui (王寵惠). By Mandate of the 13th of July, 1918, it was transformed into the Law Codification Commission (修訂法律館) with the Minister of Justice and Dr. Wang Chung Hui as Directors, the actual control of the work being in the hands of Dr. Wang, with Mr. G. Padoux, Minister Plenipotentiary, former Legislative adviser of the Siamese Government, and two Japanese jurists, as technical advisers. The Commission later on, in 1921, engaged the services of Professor J. Escarra of the Grenoble University.

The programme of the Commission included the revision of the Provisional Penal Code enacted in March, 1912, the remodelling of the Draft Civil Code and the compilation of Codes of Civil and Criminal Procedure.

The work on the Civil Code lasted several years.

The Commission first compiled a draft in 744 articles including the General Principles (Articles 1 to 223) and the

Introduction

Book on Obligations (Articles 224 to 744); then a draft on the Law of Things, in 310 articles; and finally two drafts on Family Law, one in 141 articles, one in 243 articles, and a draft on Inheritance in 225 articles.

All these drafts were printed and published in Chinese. The draft on General Principles was translated into English and French by the Chinese Commission on Extraterritoriality and published in February, 1926. The draft on Obligations was translated into French only, by the same Commission.

The Peking Ministry of Justice was contemplating to have the part on General Principles and Obligations, as revised in 1925, adopted and promulgated, but political events did not allow these projects to materialize. The Peking Government, which had deviated from constitutional legality, was weakened by internal dissensions. It was battered by the Kuomintang reformers who, being heirs to the traditions of Dr. Sun Yat Sen, the founder of the Republic, had formed in Canton an independent Nationalist Government.

With the establishment in Nanking of the National Government, the Codification Commission disappeared. Its duties were taken over by the Li Fa Yuan (立法院) the legislative organ of the Government during the tutelage period.*

The Li Fa Yuan (according to its organic law of October 20th, 1928) includes four great commissions, the most important of which is the Legislative Commission. For the compilation of the principal codes, the Li Fa Yuan established five special Commissions, viz.:

---

*Conforming with the teachings of Dr. Sun Yat Sen, the execution of the political programme of the Kuomintang must pass through three successive stages: the military period, devoted to the conquest of the country and to the elimination of the local chieftains; the tutelage period, during which the party continues in power in order to give to the citizens the civil education which is the necessary preliminary for the exercise of public liberties; and the constitutional period, beginning with which the people will directly control the Government. It is considered that the military period ended when the Nationalist armies entered Peking in July, 1928.

During the tutelage period, the power is exercised, under the direction of the Executive Council of that Party, by a State Council (whose President acts as the President of the Republic) and five controlling organs or Yuans. The Executive Yuan which supervises the several ministries, the Legislative Yuan which acts as Parliament, the Judicial Yuan which controls the administration of justice, the Examination Yuan which selects proper candidates for the various official functions, and the Control Yuan which audits the accounts of the official organs and may impeach officials. This is what is called the Five Powers system.

Introduction

Commission on Civil Codification;
Commission on Commercial Codification;
Commission on Land Legislation;
Commission on Labour Laws;
Commission on Local Administration Laws (Municipal organization of towns, boroughs and villages).

The Civil Codification Commission consists of Messrs. Foo Ping-Sheung, (傅秉常), Chairman; Chao Yeh-tang (焦易堂); Sze Shang-quan (史尚寬); Ling Ping (林彬) and Miss Soumi Cheng (鄭毓秀), as Members, with Dr. Wang Chung-hui (王寵惠), Member of the National Government, President of the Judicial Yuan, Mr. Tai Chi-tao (戴季陶), Member of the National Government, President of the Examination Yuan, and Mr. G. Padoux, Councillor of the Legislative and Judicial Yuans, as Advisers.

The Commission took up the work with remarkable energy. First, they ascertained the views of the Government on a number of points concerning the general part of the Code which could touch the essential principles of the Kuomintang. An opinion of the Central Political Council, dated December 10th, 1928, gave the necessary directions on 19 main points. The general lines being thus settled, the Commission started from the 1925 draft, took into consideration the counter drafts or amendments submitted by its members or advisers, and was able to place before the Li Fa Yuan on April 13th, 1929, an entirely remodelled text of Book I. The Li Fa Yuan, in plenary session, examined the text minutely, amended its form as well as its substance and adopted it at its sittings of the 13th, 16th, 17th, and 20th April. The President of the Yuan, His Exc. Hu Han Min, submitted it immediately to the Council of State which approved it at its 18th session of May 10th. It was promulgated on May 23rd, 1929, as the *Book on the General Principles of the Civil Code,* to come into force on October 10th, 1929, the anniversary of the beginning of the Revolution.

A *Law on the Application of the Book on the General Principles of the Civil Code,* in nineteen articles was compiled in accordance with the same procedure and was promulgated by the Council of State on September 24th, 1929. The Law

Introduction

decides how the provisions of Book I are to come into force and when they will govern the juristic relations which existed prior to its promulgation. It contains six important articles on the juristic capacity of foreigners and of foreign juristic persons, on the method of recognition of such foreign juristic persons and on the law applicable to them.

As soon as Book I was finished, the Commission began work on Book II (Obligations) and Book III (Law of Things). Same as for Book I, the Central Political Council enunciated on June 5th fifteen general principles on Obligations and on October 30th fifteen general principles relating to the Law of Things. The compilation lasted longer than for Book I; Books II and III including 714 articles whilst Book I had only 152. Book II was completed on November 1st, 1929, and transmitted to the Li Fa Yuan, which discussed, amended and adopted it at its meetings of November 5th, 6th, 7th and 8th. On November 15th Book III was finished; the Li Fa Yuan revised and adopted it on November 19th, 20th and 21st.

Book II was sanctioned by the Council of State at its 51st meeting of November 15th, 1929, and promulgated on November 21st. Book III, sanctioned at the 52nd meeting of November 22nd, was promulgated on November 30th. By ordinances of February 10th, 1930, both books were ordered to come into execution on May 5th, 1930.

Book IV on Family and Book V on Successions are being prepared and will be promulgated by the end of 1930.

III.

The work which has thus been done by the Legislative Yuan is by no means a simple revision of the Chinese draft of the year 1925. The general distribution in five books has been preserved. But the internal distribution of each of the Books has been modified; many old provisions have been omitted or altered and many new ones have been added, and a new spirit has permeated the whole structure.

The 1925 draft went into minute details and its form was exceedingly scientific. On these two points a thorough reform has been accomplished.

Introduction

First of all, it was thought that in such a vast country as China, extending over the major part of inhabited Asia, and whose population exceeds four hundred millions, it was impossible to impose uniform minute rules on every sort of human activities. Room was to be left for the application of local customs. There were in the 1925 draft a number of provisions of secondary importance which are commonly called "interpretative provisions." They are to be found in most of the codes and are intended to supplement omissions in the documents or silence of the parties. These "style clauses" are supposed to represent the presumed intentions of the people concerned, what they would have said or what they would have done if they had expressly shown their will. Most of these provisions have been left out, the diversity of local practices showing sufficiently that no uniform given formula could fulfil everywhere the requisite aims, and that the "style clauses" differ in China from place to place. On many other points, the application of local customs differing from the Code provisions was expressly reserved: this is particularly noticeable in the Third Book on Rights over things which deals with the various forms of tenure of land. It was the wish of the Commission that many traditional agricultural customs, which had grown out of the geographical or economic conditions of particular districts should be preserved so long as they were not contrary to public order or good morals.

On the other hand, the scope of the Code was enlarged so as to make it a *Civil and Commercial Code* the rules of which would be applicable to both Civil and Commercial cases.

As is well known to every student of law, the distinction between Civil and Commercial Law is due to historical causes of European origin such as the existence of a merchant class which had traditional customs of its own, and of commercial courts to which commercial cases only were amenable. In many countries, there is the additional reason that bankruptcy proceedings can be taken only against tradesmen, excluding other private individuals.

No such causes exist in China. The Chinese merchants do combine into guilds and chambers of commerce for the protection of their professional interests, but they do not form

Introduction

a caste or a class of their own and the same civil law, all through Chinese legal history, has been applied to merchants and non-merchants by one and the same set of Courts. There have never been special commercial tribunals. And bankruptcy proceedings, or what would correspond to bankruptcy proceedings, in the traditional Chinese precedure would apply to any person who is unable to meet his liabilities, whether such person be a merchant or not. The policy of the Kuomintang Party being the political and social unification of the Republic and of her people, there is no idea of introducing now in China a sort of class distinction which she had never known.

Tendencies in other Countries are pointing in the same direction. The distinction between merchants and non-merchants is rapidly disappearing all over the world with the progress of democratization and with the economic necessities which at present compel every person to work and to do business in order to earn his living.

The discrimination between commercial acts and non-commercial acts, between commercial cases and non-commercial cases has become, in every country where it has been retained, a purely technical distinction, involving intricate points of jurisdiction, procedure and application of law, the discussion of which is to nobody's advantage.

It was therefore decided to make the new Civil Code a Code for *Civil* and *Commercial* cases, and the adjective *Civil,* when used in its title and in its context, must be understood as meaning *Civil* by opposition to *Penal* and as including *Civil* and *Commercial* law.

The text of the General Principles had therefore to be modelled so as to cover a larger field; the same for the General Provisions on Obligations in Book II. In the part of Book II concerning Specific Contracts additions had to be made to the provisions on Sale for instance, so as to make them suitable for sales transactions between merchants as well as for other sales. New Titles were introduced dealing with Contracts which are considered as having a decided commercial character, such as Current Account, Brokerage, Commission Agency, etc.

xvii

Introduction

Not all the commercial matters were however inserted in the Code. It was decided to leave some of the more important ones to be dealt with by separate special Laws. These matters are:

> Negotiable Instruments,
> Insurance,
> Commercial Companies,
> Maritime Law.

The decision of the Government to have these matters governed by laws outside the Code was prompted by four reasons:

(*a*) These are matters where the practice of the business world is rapidly evolving, and where amendments may be necessary from time to time. It is always easier to amend a law than to amend a Code.

(*b*) Matters like the maritime law contain a large proportion of administrative rules which would be out of place in a Civil Code.

(*c*) Elaborate drafts had been already prepared on these subjects in the form of separate laws; it was easier and it would save time to revise them as such rather than to insert them in the Code.

(*d*) The insertion of the above four items in the Code would have made the Code too bulky and too difficult to handle.

The parts of the commercial law which have been left out of the Code were studied with great care by the Commission on Commercial Codification. The result of their labour has been the compilation and adoption of the following laws:—

> Law on Negotiable Instruments, promulgated October 30th, 1929.

> Law on Commercial Companies, promulgated December 26th, 1929.

> Law on Maritime Commerce, promulgated December 30th, 1929.

> Law on Insurance, promulgated December 30th, 1929.

With regard to the wording of the articles, scientific phraseology has been discarded in the Code as far as circumstances admit. Those who read the Chinese text will probably

Introduction

find that in some cases its phraseology is intricate and somewhat unusual. But this could not be avoided: to render into Chinese ideas or formulas taken from the western legal language requires the coining of new expressions which, for some years to come, will bear an unfamiliar aspect to the ordinary reader. The putting into Chinese of technical rules so easily expressed in legal French, German or English, but for which there exist no corresponding expressions in the Chinese vocabulary, however rich this vocabulary may be, has proved one of the hardest tasks of the Commission.

V.

Coming now to the spirit of the Code, we might say that it is an adaptation of the best of western legal science to the needs of renovated China.

The primitive draft, as explained above, under the influence of the members of the original Commission, who had been educated in Japan, and of the Commission's Japanese advisers, was following rather closely the lines of the Japanese Civil Code of 1898, and of the German Code of 1896 from which the Japanese legislators had drawn their inspiration.

But progress has been made during the last 30 years in the science of codification. Switzerland produced its Civil Code in 1907 and the revised edition of its Code on Obligations in 1911. The Soviet Government gave Russia a legislation based on communistic principles, including, *inter alia,* a Code on Family, published first in 1918, revised in 1922, and a Civil Code (Obligations, Real Rights and Commercial Law) published in 1922. Siam, a small but progressive country of the Far East, whose customs are partly derived from Chinese origin, has been enacting a Civil and Commercial Code, parts of which have appeared in the years 1923-25. Turkey has put into force a complete set of modern Codes, including a Civil Code, a Code on Obligations and a Commercial Code, all three published in 1926. Italy is considering the revision of her Commercial Code, a draft for such revision having been prepared in 1925. A commission consisting of noted French and Italian jurists compiled in 1927 the Draft of an identical

xix

Introduction

Franco-Italian Code on Obligations and Contracts, to take the place of the respective French and Italian Codes on the matter. This Draft constitutes an up-to-date revision of the Code Napoleon and is one of the most remarkable products of modern legal science.

All this material has been carefully studied by the Members of the Commission on Civil Codification. Whilst it is impossible to describe in detail how the work of the Committee has been influenced in that respect, it may be said that the Committee has taken into consideration the innovations of many of the above mentioned Codes whenever they were tending to give better expression to an existing rule of law, or to introduce provisions in harmony with the democratic principles of the Kuomintang.

VI.

In his philosophical and political writings, Dr. Sun Yat Sen has on several occasions brought out the point that the old Chinese conception of law was already ahead of that of the Western legists. Occidental legislation is essentially individualistic; it is intended to protect the rights of the individual and to let them freely develop. The traditional Chinese legislation, on the contrary, is *familiar*; it subordinates the activities of the individual to the interests of his family. The new Chinese legislation, based on the Three Principles, racial, democratic and economic, is going one step further and will have a deliberate social character. Comparing the natural tendency of man towards expansion to centrifugal force, the tendency of society towards cohesion to centripetal force, Dr. Sun foresees the harmonious future of humanity in a combination of the two tendencies, the latter rather taking precedency over the former. The individual must seek his own gratification in such development of his own natural abilities as is most likely to contribute to the general welfare.

The Kuomintang doctrine considers therefore men not as self-contained entities, but in relation to the society which they form. It assigns to them rights and duties only in so far as the exercise of such rights and duties tends to the pacific and

Introduction

orderly progress of the community. It restricts their activities when they would be harmful to the group. Rights and morals in the Kuomintang doctrine are purely social notions, which may eventually be subject to evolution, just as society itself evolves.

Starting from the general principle of a social equilibrium to be preserved between the interests of the individual and the interests of the group, the Kuomintang Party proposes first, in positive legislation, to secure a better and more equitable distribution of wealth among the individuals.

The views expressed on this subject are not particular to the Kuomintang. They may be found in the political programmes of all the advanced democratic parties of the world. But the starting point is different. Whilst in Europe and America they try to adjust the opposing interests of different classes of population, the Kuomintang tries to make the notion of social order prevail. In practice the legal forms through which the two conceptions are expressed do not differ, and in order to execute the intention of the party the Commission had only to combine on that matter precedent derived from various foreign legislations.

This is by no means an exclusive Kuomintang principle. Advanced democracies have already framed laws to that effect, and China had only to combine on that matter precedent derived from European or American legislations.

For securing a more equitable distribution of wealth among the people, it is essential that the less fortunate elements of the population be protected against the hardships which they would suffer if the strictest rules of law were always indiscriminately applied. *Summum jus, summa injuria* says the old Roman dictum. The Code introduces an element of humanity by allowing the Courts, when passing judgment on civil claims, to take into consideration the respective circumstances of the debtor and of the creditor and to grant time to the debtor for the performance of his obligation. Article 391 on Sale by Instalments, Article 442 on Lease, Article 836 on Superficies, Article 846 on Yung-tien, etc., may be quoted as apt illustrations of this protective tendency.

xxi

Introduction

The Labour Laws and Land Laws which are now under consideration will contain further provisions for preventing exploitation of servants by masters and of tenants by landlords.

Article 74 is another case in point. It provides that in case of a juristic act whereby a person profiting by the difficulties, indiscretion or inexperience of another obtains an advantage exceeding the consideration for it to such an extent that the unfairness of the transaction is obvious, the Court may cancel the juristic act or reduce the obligation.

As a complement of the whole system of protection the Code decides in its Article 148 that a right cannot be exercised for the main purpose of causing injury to another person, thus doing away with the antique theory which defines ownership as the right to use and to abuse the thing owned. Private property rights are sanctioned by the principles of the late Dr. Sun, but on condition that in their exercise due care be taken to respect other persons' rights and to act in a way which is not injurious to the community at large. Several provisions of Book III on Rights over Things, such as Articles 733, 774, 786, 790, etc., are inspired with this view, on which the whole of the Chinese land legislation is to be based.

FOO PING-SHEUNG.

Table of Contents

Preface	v
Foreword	vii
Introduction	ix

BOOK I.—GENERAL PRINCIPLES

Chapter I. Application and Interpretation of Laws	3
Chapter II. Persons	5
Title I.—Natural Persons	3
Title II.—Juristic Persons	9
Part 1.—General Provisions	9
Part 2.—Associations	12
Part 3.—Foundations	16
Chapter III. Things	19
Chapter IV. Juristic Acts	21
Title I.—General Provisions	21
Title II.—Disposing Capacity	22
Title III.—Declaration of Intention	25
Title IV.—Conditions—Time of Commencement and Ending	28
Title V.—Agency	29
Title VI.—Void and Voidable Acts	31
Chapter V. Dates and Periods	33
Chapter VI. Extinctive Prescription	35
Chapter VII. Exercise of Rights	41

BOOK II.—OBLIGATIONS

Chapter I. General Provisions	45
Title I.—Sources of Obligations	45
Part 1.—Contracts	45
Part 2.—Conferring of Authority of Agency	48
Part 3.—Management of Affairs Without Mandate	49
Part 4.—Undue Enrichment	51
Part 5.—Wrongful Acts	53

xxiii

Table of Contents—*continued*

Title II.—Object of Obligations 58
Title III.—Effects of Obligations 63
    Part 1.—Performance 63
    Part 2.—Default 65
    Part 3.—Preservation 67
    Part 4.—Contracts 68
Title IV.—Plurality of Creditors and Debtors . . 75
Title V.—Transfer of Obligations 80
Title VI.—Extinction of Obligations 84
    Part 1.—General Provisions 84
    Part 2.—Performance 84
    Part 3.—Lodgment 88
    Part 4.—Set-Off 90
    Part 5.—Release 91
    Part 6.—Merger 32

CHAPTER II. PARTICULAR KINDS OF OBLIGATIONS 93

Title I.—Sale 93
    Part 1.—General Provisions 93
    Part 2.—Effects of Sale 94
    Part 3.—Redemption 101
    Part 4.—Particular Kinds of Sale 102
Title II.—Exchange 105
Title III.—Current Account 106
Title IV.—Gift 107
Title V.—Lease 110
Title VI.—Loan 120
    Part 1.—Loan for Use 120
    Part 2.—Loan for Consumption 122
Title VII.—Hire of Services 125
Title VIII.—Hire of Work 127
Title IX.—Publication 134
Title X.—Mandate 138
Title XI.—Manager and Commercial Agents . . 144
Title XII.—Brokerage 147
Title XIII.—Commission Agency 150
Title XIV.—Deposit 153
Title XV.—Warehousing 159
Title XVI.—Carriage 162
    Part 1.—General Provisions 162

Table of Contents—*continued*

Part 2.—Carriage of Goods 162
Part 3.—Carriage of Passengers 168
Title XVII.—Forwarding Agency 170
Title XVIII.—Partnership 172
Title XIX.—Sleeping Partnership 179
Title XX.—Orders of Payment.. 181
Title XXI.—Obligations to Bearer 184
Title XXII.—Life Interests 187
Title XXIII.—Compromise 188
Title XXIV.—Suretyship 189

BOOK III.—RIGHTS OVER THINGS

CHAPTER I. GENERAL PROVISIONS 195
CHAPTER II. OWNERSHIP 197
Title I.—General Provisions 197
Title II.—Ownership of Immovables 199
Title III.—Ownership of Movables 207
Title IV.—Co-Ownership 210
CHAPTER III. SUPERFICIES 215
CHAPTER IV. YUNG-TIEN 217
CHAPTER V. SERVITUDES 219
CHAPTER VI. MORTGAGES 221
CHAPTER VII. PLEDGE 227
Title I.—Pledge of Movables 227
Title II.—Pledge of Rights 230
CHAPTER VIII. DIEN 233
CHAPTER IX. RIGHT OF RETENTION.. 237
CHAPTER X. POSSESSION 241

LAWS OF APPLICATION

LAW GOVERNING THE APPLICATION OF THE GENERAL
PRINCIPLES OF THE CIVIL CODE 249
LAW GOVERNING THE APPLICATION OF THE BOOK OF
OBLIGATIONS OF THE CIVIL CODE 257
LAW GOVERNING THE APPLICATION OF THE BOOK OF
RIGHTS OVER THINGS OF THE CIVIL CODE 263

INDEX 271

THE CIVIL CODE

of

THE REPUBLIC

OF CHINA

Book I

GENERAL PRINCIPLES

CHAPTER I

———

RULES FOR THE APPLICATION
OF LAWS

Article 1.—In civil matters if there is no provision of law applicable to a case, the case shall be decided according to custom. If there is no such custom, the case shall be decided in accordance with the general principles of law.

Article 2.—A custom is applicable in civil matters only when it is not contrary to public order or good morals.

Article 3.—Whenever a writing is required by law, it is not necessary that it be written by the person from whom it is required, but it must be signed by him.

If a person uses a seal in lieu of signature, the affixing of such seal is equivalent to a signature.

If a finger-print, cross or other mark is used in lieu of signature, it is equivalent to a signature provided that it is certified on the document by the signature of two witnesses.

Article 4.—Whenever a sum or quantity is expressed at the same time in characters and in figures, if the two expressions do not agree and the Court cannot ascertain which of them represented the real intention of the parties, the expression in characters shall be held good.

Chapter I   *Rules for the Application of Laws*

THE CHINESE CIVIL CODE

Article 5.—Whenever a sum or quantity is expressed several times in characters or several times in figures, if the several expressions do not agree and the Court cannot ascertain which of them represented the real intention of the parties, the lowest expression shall be held good.

CHAPTER II

PERSONS

TITLE I.—NATURAL PERSONS

Article 6.—The legal capacity of a person begins from the moment of birth and terminates at the moment of death.

Article 7.—A child *en ventre sa mere* is considered as if he were already born in respect to the protection of his personal interest, provided that he was subsequently born alive.

Article 8.—A missing person may be declared dead by the Court upon the application of any interested party if he has disappeared for more than ten years.

If the missing person was over seventy years of age, he may be declared dead if he has disappeared for more than five years.

If the missing person was in special peril of his life he may be declared dead if he has disappeared for more than three years.

Article 9.—A person who has been declared dead is presumed to have been dead from the date fixed in the judicial decree.

In the absence of proof to the contrary, the date of death specified in the preceding paragraph shall be the

Chapter II *Persons*

The Chinese Civil Code

date of the expiration of the period fixed in the preceding article.

Article 10.—The property of the missing person, after his disappearance and up to the declaration of death, shall be administered in accordance with the regulations, governing non-contentious matters.

Article 11.—If several persons have perished in a common peril and it is not possible to ascertain which of them perished first, they are presumed to have died simultaneously.

Article 12.—Majority begins with the completion of the twentieth year of age.

Article 13.—A minor who has not completed his seventh year of age has no disposing capacity.

A minor who is over seven years of age has a limited disposing capacity.

A minor who marries acquires thereby the disposing capacity.

Article 14.—Persons who are in such a state of unconsciousness or feeblemindedness that they are unable to manage their own affairs, may be interdicted by the Court on the application of the person himself, or his spouse, or two of his nearest relatives.

The interdiction shall be revoked if the cause thereof disappears.

Article 15.—Interdicted persons have no disposing capacity.

Article 16.—No person shall be allowed to waive his legal capacity or his disposing capacity.

Title I   *Natural Persons*

ARTICLES 10 TO 22

Article 17.—No person shall be allowed to waive his liberty.

Liberty may not be restricted in a manner contrary to public order or good morals.

Article 18.—If any right appertaining to one's personality is unlawfully infringed, application may be made to the Court for the suppression of the infringement.

Under the above circumstances an action for damages or for solatium may be brought only in those cases which are specifically provided by law.

Article 19.—If the right to the use of one's name is unlawfully infringed, application may be made to the Court for the suppression of the infringement and for damages.

Article 20.—A person who resides in a place with the intention of remaining there permanently, establishes his domicile at that place.

A person may not have more than one domicile at one and the same time.

Article 21.—The domicile of a person incapable of disposing or limited in disposing capacity is the domicile of his statutory agent.

Article 22.—In either of the following cases a person's residence is deemed to be his domicile:—

  1. Where his domicile is unknown;
  2. Where he has no domicile in China, except when otherwise provided by law regarding the *lex domicilii*.

Chapter II   Persons

THE CHINESE CIVIL CODE

Article 23.—If a person has chosen a residence for a special purpose, the residence is deemed to be his domicile for that purpose.

Article 24.—Domicile is lost if discontinued with the intention of abandoning it.

TITLE II.—JURISTIC PERSONS

Part 1.—General Provisions

Article 25.—A juristic person can exist only in accordance with the provisions of this Code or of any other law.

Article 26.—Within the limits prescribed by law or ordinances, a juristic person has the capacity of enjoying rights and assuming obligations with the exception of those rights and obligations which appertain exclusively to natural persons.

Article 27.—A juristic person must have at least one director.

For the management of its affairs, a juristic person is represented by its directors.

No limitation placed upon the right of representation of a director can be set up against *bonâ fide* third parties.

Article 28.—A juristic person is jointly liable with the wrongdoer for the injury done by its directors or employees in the performance of their duties.

Article 29.—The domicile of a juristic person is at the place where it has its principal office.

Article 30.—A juristic person cannot come into existence unless registered with the competent authorities.

Article 31.—A registered juristic person cannot, as against third parties, avail itself of unregistered matters which should have been registered, or of unregistered changes in registered matters.

THE CHINESE CIVIL CODE

Article 32.—The activities of a juristic person which has been authorized are subject to the control of the competent authorities. The competent authorities may examine its financial situation, and ascertain whether the conditions of the authorization and other legal requirements have been complied with.

Article 33.—The director of an authorized juristic person who disobeys a supervising order of, or obstructs an inspection by the competent authorities, may be punished with a fine not exceeding five hundred *yuan*.

Article 34.—If a juristic person violates any of the conditions under which the authorization has been granted, the authorization may be revoked by the competent authorities.

Article 35.—When the assets of a juristic person are insufficient to meet its liabilities, the directors shall forthwith apply to the Court for a declaration of bankruptcy.

If injury has been caused to the creditors of a juristic person through failure to apply to the Court for a declaration of bankruptcy, as provided in the preceding paragraph, the director who is in fault shall be responsible for damages.

Article 36.—Whenever the object or the activities of a juristic person are found to be contrary to law, public order or good morals, the Court may order the dissolution of the juristic person on the application of the competent authorities, the public procurator or any interested person.

Title II   *Juristic Persons*

ARTICLES 32 TO 43

Article 37.—After the dissolution of a juristic person the liquidation is effected by its directors, unless otherwise provided by the constitution or by a special resolution of the general meeting of members.

Article 38.—When the appointment of liquidators under the preceding article is impossible, the Court may appoint liquidators on the application of an interested party.

Article 39.—All liquidators may be removed by the Court whenever the Court deems it necessary.

Article 40.—It shall be the duty of the liquidators:—
1. to wind up pending business;
2. to collect the assets and discharge the liabilities;
3. to deliver the surplus of assets, if any, to the persons entitled thereto.

Until the liquidation is completed, the dissolved juristic person is deemed to continue to exist in so far as is necessary for the purpose of the liquidation.

Article 41.—Unless otherwise provided by these General Provisions, the liquidation shall be carried out, as far as possible, in conformity with the legal provisions concerning the liquidation of limited companies.

Article 42.—The liquidation of a juristic person shall be subject to the supervision of the Court.

The Court may from time to time make such inspection as is necessary for the supervision.

Article 43.—A liquidator who disobeys a supervising order of the Court or who obstructs an inspection by the

Chapter II   *Persons*

THE CHINESE CIVIL CODE

Court may be punished with a fine not exceeding five hundred *yuan*.

Article 44.—After the juristic person has been dissolved and its liabilities discharged, the remaining assets shall be assigned in conformity with the constitution or with the resolution of the general meeting of members.

In the absence of any such provision in the constitution or of a resolution of the general meeting of members, the remaining assets devolve upon the local autonomous institutions of the place in which the juristic person is domiciled.

Part 2.—Associations

Article 45.—An association whose object is to make profits acquires juristic personality in accordance with the provisions of special laws.

Article 46.—An association whose object is for the promotion of public welfare must, prior to registering itself, be authorized by the competent authorities.

Article 47.—In order to form an association a constitution must be drawn up which shall contain the following particulars:—

1. Object;
2. Name;
3. Provisions relating to the appointment and dismissal of directors;
4. The conditions and formalities for calling the general meeting of members, and the method for the authentification of its resolutions;

Title II   *Juristic Persons*

ARTICLES 44 TO 49

5. Provisions concerning the contributions of the members;

6. Provisions concerning the acquisition and loss of membership.

Article 48.—In order to form an association the following particulars shall be registered:—

1. Object;

2. Name;

3. The principal and branch offices;

4. The names and domiciles of its directors;

5. The total amount of its assets;

6. If the association has been authorized, the date and particulars of the authorization;

7. The method of contributing property, if such method has been fixed;

8. The limitation of the power of the directors to represent the association, if such limitation has been made;

9. The period of its existence, if such period has been fixed.

The association shall be registered by the directors with the competent authorities of the principal office and branch offices. A copy of the constitution shall be annexed to the petition for registration.

Article 49.—The constitution may provide for the organisation of the association and the relations of the

Chapter II   *Persons*

THE CHINESE CIVIL CODE

association with its members, provided that nothing therein shall contravene the provisions of Articles 50 to 58.

Article 50.—The general meeting of members of an association is the organ in which the supreme power of the association is vested.

The following matters shall be decided by a resolution of the general meeting of members:—

1. Alterations in the constitution;
2. Appointment and dismissal of directors;
3. Supervision of the directors in the performance of their duties;
4. Expulsion of members for a proper cause.

Article 51.—The general meeting of members shall be called by the directors.

If over one-tenth of the members of an association request the directors to call a general meeting, specifying the objects of the meeting and the reasons for its convocation, the directors must call the meeting accordingly.

If no general meeting is called by the directors within one month after the receipt of the above request, the members who have made the request may call the meeting, with the authorization of the Court.

Article 52.—Unless otherwise provided in this Code, a resolution of the general meeting of members is valid if passed by a majority vote of the members present.

Members shall have equal votes.

Article 53.—A resolution involving an alteration in the constitution of an association can be passed only at a

| *Title II* | *Juristic Persons* |

ARTICLES 50 TO 56

meeting at which the majority of the members of the association are present, and by a majority of more than three-fourths of the members present; or when more than two-thirds of the members of the association declare in writing their consent thereto.

If an association has been authorized, a resolution involving an alteration in its constitution must be approved by the competent authorities.

Article 54.—Members may withdraw from the association at any time unless according to the constitution they have to remain until the expiration of the business year, or unless previous notice of withdrawal is required by the constitution.

The period of notice as mentioned above cannot exceed six months.

Article 55.—A retired or dismissed member has no right over the property of the association unless it is otherwise provided in the constitution of an association whose object is not for the promotion of public welfare.

The above mentioned member continues to be liable for his share of the contribution which has become due before his retirement or dismissal.

Article 56.—When a resolution passed by a general meeting of members is contrary to law or ordinances or to the constitution of the association, any member who has not assented thereto may apply to the Court for having the resolution declared null and void.

The application as mentioned above must be made within three months from the date of the resolution.

| *Chapter II* | *Persons* |

The Chinese Civil Code

Article 57.—An association may be dissolved at any time by a resolution of the general meeting of members passed by a majority vote of more than two-thirds of all the members of the association.

Article 58.—An association may be dissolved by an order of the Court on the application of any interested person when circumstances are such that it cannot be managed any more in accordance with its constitution.

Part 3.—Foundations

Article 59.—A foundation must, before registration, be authorized by the competent authorities.

Article 60.—In order to constitute a foundation an act of endowment must be drawn up, except in the case of donation by will.

The act of endowment must specify the object of the foundation and the property donated.

Article 61.—In order to constitute a foundation, the following particulars shall be registered:—

1. Object;
2. Name;
3. The principal and branch offices;
4. The total amount of its assets;
5. The date of the authorization;
6. The names and domiciles of the directors;
7. The limitation of the power of the directors to represent the foundation, if such limitation has been made;

Title II	*Juristic Persons*

ARTICLES 57 TO 65

8. The period of its existence, if such period has been fixed.

The foundation shall be registered by the directors with the competent authorities of the principal office and branch offices. A copy of the act of endowment must be annexed to the petition for registration.

Article 62.—The organization and method of administration of the foundation shall be determined by the founder in the act of endowment.

If the organization as provided in the act of endowment is insufficient or if the important provisions are lacking concerning the method of administration, the Court may on the application of any interested party take such measures as may be necessary.

Article 63.—For the purpose of maintaining the object of the foundation or of preserving its property, the Court may modify the organization of the foundation on the application of the founder, or the directors, or any interested party.

Article 64.—If the directors act contrary to the act of endowment, their acts may on the application of any interested party be declared null and void by the Court.

Article 65.—If by reason of changes in the circumstances the object of the foundation cannot be carried out, the competent authorities may, after taking into consideration the intention of the founder, alter the object of the foundation or the essentials of its organization, or dissolve the foundation.

CHAPTER III

——

THINGS

Article 66.—Immovables are land and things permanently affixed thereto.

The products of an immovable constitute a part of the immovable so long as they are not separated therefrom.

Article 67.—All things other than immovables mentioned in preceding articles are movables.

Article 68.—Accessories are things which, without being component parts of the principal thing, are intended to facilitate its utilization and belong to the same owner. But, if there is a special custom prevailing in trade, such custom shall be followed.

The disposal of the principal thing extends to its accessories.

Article 69.—Natural fruits are fruits, offspring of animals, and such other produce as may be obtained from the thing consistently with the use for which the thing is intended.

Legal fruits are interest, rent and other profits obtained by virtue of a legal relation.

Article 70.—A person who is entitled to the natural

Chapter III	Things

THE CHINESE CIVIL CODE

fruits of a thing acquires during the existence of his right the fruits which are separated from the thing.

A person who is entitled to the legal fruits of a thing acquires them in proportion to the number of days during which his right exists.

Chapter IV

JURISTIC ACTS

Title I.—General Provisions

Article 71.—A juristic act which is contrary to an imperative or prohibitive provision of law is void, unless nullity is not necessarily implied.

Article 72.—A juristic act which is contrary to public order or good morals is void.

Article 73.—A juristic act which is not in the form prescribed by law is void, unless otherwise provided by law.

Article 74.—In the case of a juristic act whereby a person profiting by the difficulties, indiscretion or inexperience of another causes to be delivered or promised pecuniary advantages to such an extent that having regard to the concomitant circumstances, the unfairness of the transaction is obvious, the Court may, on the application of the injured party, cancel the juristic act or reduce the prestation.

The application as mentioned above must be made within one year from the date of the juristic act.

Chapter IV *Juristic Acts*

THE CHINESE CIVIL CODE

TITLE II.—DISPOSING CAPACITY

Article 75.—The declaration of intention of a person incapable of disposing is void. A declaration is also void which is made by a person who, though not incapable of disposing, is in a condition of absence of discernment or mental disorder.

Article 76.—For the making or receiving of a declaration of intention a person incapable of disposing is represented by his statutory agent.

Article 77.—Where a person limited in disposing capacity makes or receives a declaration of intention, the approval of the statutory agent is necessary, unless the declaration of intention relates to the mere acquisition of a legal advantage, or to the necessaries of life according to the age and social standing of the person limited in disposing capacity.

Article 78.—A unilateral act which a person limited in disposing capacity enters into without the approval of his statutory agent is void.

Article 79.—If a person limited in disposing capacity enters into a contract without the approval of his statutory agent, the contract is effective only upon ratification by the statutory agent.

Article 80.—The other party to the contract mentioned in the preceding article may fix a period, not less than one month, and request the statutory agent to declare definitely within such period whether or not he ratifies the contract.

Title II   *Disposing Capacity*

ARTICLES 75 TO 85

If the statutory agent does not give a definite answer within the above-mentioned period, the ratification is deemed to have been refused.

Article 81.—When the cause for which a person's disposing capacity is limited has disappeared, his ratification of the contract which he has previously entered into has the same effect as that of his statutory agent.

The provision of the preceding article applies *mutatis mutandis* to the case provided for in the preceding paragraph.

Article 82.—Before ratification of the contract made by a person limited in disposing capacity, the other party is entitled to rescind it, unless he knew, at the time when it was entered into, that the approval of the statutory agent had not been given.

Article 83.—A juristic act done by a person limited in disposing capacity is valid if such person by using fraudulent means has induced the other party to believe that he had full capacity or that he had obtained the approval of his statutory agent.

Article 84.—If the statutory agent of a person limited in disposing capacity has authorized the latter to dispose of a certain property, the person is capable of disposing of the said property.

Article 85.—If the statutory agent of a person limited in disposing capacity has authorized the latter to carry on a business independently, such person has full disposing capacity in respect to the said business.

The authorization may be revoked, or restricted by

Chapter IV   *Juristic Acts*

THE CHINESE CIVIL CODE

the statutory agent if the person limited in disposing capacity proves himself to be incapable of carrying on the business thus authorized.

Title III *Declaration of Intention*

ARTICLES 86 TO 90

TITLE III.—DECLARATION OF INTENTION

Article 86.—A declaration of intention is not void by reason of the fact that the declarant did not intend to be bound by it, unless such fact was known to the other party.

Article 87.—A fictitious declaration of intention made by the declarant in collusion with the other party is void, but the fact of its being void cannot be set up against a *bonâ fide* third party.

If the fictitious declaration of intention was intended to cover another juristic act, the provisions of law concerning such other juristic act shall apply.

Article 88.—A declaration of intention may be avoided by the declarant if he was acting under a mistake as to the contents of the declaration of intention, or had he known the real state of affairs, he would not have made the declaration; provided that the mistake or the ignorance of the real state of affairs was not due to the declarant's own fault.

A mistake concerning the qualifications of the other party or the nature of a thing which, in commercial transactions, are regarded as essential, shall be deemed a mistake as to the contents of the declaration of intention.

Article 89.—A declaration of intention which has been incorrectly transmitted by the person or institution employed for its transmission may be avoided under the same conditions as provided for in the preceding article.

Article 90.—The right of avoidance provided in the above two articles must be exercised within one year from the date of the declaration.

Chapter IV   *Juristic Acts*

THE CHINESE CIVIL CODE

Article 91.—If a declaration of intention is avoided under Article 88 or Article 89, the declarant shall make compensation for any damage which the other party or any third party may have sustained by relying upon the validity of the declaration, unless the injured party knew, or had the means of knowing, of the ground on which the declaration was voidable.

Article 92.—If a declaration of intention is procured by fraud or by duress the declarant may avoid it. If a third party was guilty of the fraud the declaration may be avoided only if the other party knew, or had the means of knowing, of the real state of affairs.

The avoidance of a declaration of intention on the ground of fraud cannot be set up against a *bonâ fide* third party.

Article 93.—The right of avoidance under the preceding article must be exercised within one year from the date when the fraud was discovered or when the duress ceased. But it cannot be exercised when ten years have elapsed since the making of the declaration of intention.

Article 94.—A declaration of intention *inter presentes** becomes effective at the moment when the person to whom it is made understands it well.

Article 95.—A declaration of intention *inter absentes* becomes effective at the moment when the notification of the declaration reaches the other party, unless a

---

* TRANSLATORS' NOTE.—For lack of a better expression, the Chinese characters " 對 話 人 " is here translated as *inter presentes*. It should be noted, however, that the Chinese characters include persons who, though not strictly *inter presentes,* communicate with each other by telephone.

Title III   *Declaration of Intention*

ARTICLES 91 TO 98

notification of revocation reaches such other party previously or simultaneously.

The fact that after the despatch of the notification of the declaration the declarant dies, or becomes incapable of disposing, or is limited in disposing capacity, shall not impair the validity of the declaration of intention.

Article 96.—A declaration of intention made to a person incapable of disposing or limited in disposing capacity becomes effective when the notification of the declaration reaches the statutory agent.

Article 97.—If a declarant, due to no fault on his part, is ignorant of the name and residence of the other party the notification of the declaration may be effected by service by public notice in accordance with the provisions of the Code of Civil Procedure.

Article 98.—In the interpretation of a declaration of intention the true intention of the parties must be sought rather than the literal meaning of the words or expressions.

Chapter IV *Juristic Acts*

THE CHINESE CIVIL CODE

TITLE IV.—CONDITIONS—TIME OF COMMENCEMENT AND ENDING

Article 99.—A juristic act subject to a condition precedent becomes effective on the fulfilment of the condition.

A juristic act subject to a condition subsequent ceases to be effective on the fulfilment of the condition.

If, according to the special agreement of the parties the consequences of the fulfilment of the condition shall take place at another time than the time of fulfilment, such special agreement shall govern.

Article 100.—In the case of a juristic act entered into subject to a condition, the person who has, during the time pending the fulfilment, done any act diminishing the advantages which the other party would have derived from the fulfilment of the condition, is responsible for any damage resulting therefrom.

Article 101.—If the fulfilment of a condition is prevented by improper means by the party to whose disadvantage it would operate, the condition is deemed to have been fulfilled.

If the fulfilment of the condition is brought about by improper means by the party to whose advantage it would operate, the condition is deemed not to have been fulfilled.

Article 102.—A juristic act subject to a time for its commencement becomes effective when the time arrives.

A juristic act subject to a time for its termination ceases to be effective when the time arrives.

In cases under the two preceding paragraphs, the provision of Article 100 applies *mutatis mutandis*.

Title V *Agency*

Articles 99 to 107

Title V.—Agency

Article 103.—A declaration of intention which an agent makes in the name of the principal within the scope of his delegated authority takes effect directly both in favour of or against the principal.

The provision of the preceding paragraph applies *mutatis mutandis* if a declaration of intention required to be made to the principal is made to his agent.

Article 104.—The validity of a declaration of intention made by or to an agent is not impaired by the fact that he is limited in disposing capacity.

Article 105.—In so far as the legal effectiveness of a declaration of intention of an agent is vitiated by defective intention, by fraud or by duress, or by knowledge or by culpable ignorance of certain circumstances, the existence or non-existence of the fact shall be determined with regard to the agent. But if the agent derives his authority from a juristic act and the declaration of intention was made according to definite instructions of the principal, the existence or non-existence of the fact shall be determined with regard to the principal.

Article 106.—Without the consent of the principal, an agent may not enter into a juristic act in the name of his principal with himself in his own name, nor may he, as agent of a third party, enter into a juristic act in the name of the principal with such third party, unless the juristic act consists exclusively in the fulfilment of an obligation.

Article 107.—No limitation or revocation of the

Chapter IV   *Juristic Acts*

THE CHINESE CIVIL CODE

power conferred on an agent can be set up against a *bonâ fide* third party unless the ignorance of the third party is due to his fault.

Article 108.—The power of agency is terminated according to the legal relation upon which its creation is based.

The power of agency is revocable during the existence of the legal relation upon which its creation is based, unless according to the nature of the legal relation it cannot be revoked.

Article 109.—At the termination of the power of agency the agent has to return the written power of agency to the party who gave it; he has no right of retention on it.

Article 110.—Whoever not having authority as agent, enters into a juristic act as agent is responsible for damages to the other party in good faith.

Title VI   *Void and Voidable Acts*

Articles 108 to 116

Title VI.—Void and Voidable Acts

Article 111.—If part of a juristic act is void, the whole juristic act is void, but if the juristic act could exist excluding the void part, the other part remains valid.

Article 112.—If a void juristic act satisfies the requirement of a different juristic act, the latter is valid if according to the circumstances it may be assumed that its validity would have been intended by the parties on knowing of the invalidity of the former.

Article 113.—A party who at the moment when a void juristic act was entered into knew or had the means of knowing that it was void, is bound to restore the state of things to its former condition, or to make good any injury resulting therefrom.

Article 114.—If a voidable juristic act is avoided, it is deemed to have been void *ab initio*.

If its voidability was known or ought to have been known to the parties concerned, the provision of the preceding article applies *mutatis mutandis* to the avoidance of the juristic act.

Article 115.—If a voidable juristic act is ratified it is deemed to have been valid from the moment when the juristic act was entered into, uness it is otherwise agreed upon.

Article 116.—An avoidance or ratification is made by a declaration of intention.

If the other party is known the declaration of intention is to be made to him.

Chapter IV   *Juristic Acts*

THE CHINESE CIVIL CODE

Article 117.—If the validity of a juristic act depends upon the consent of a third party, the giving or the refusal of the consent may be declared as well to the one as to the other party.

Article 118.—A disposition affecting any object which is made by a person without title is effective only upon the ratification of the person entitled.

The disposition is valid *ab initio,* if the person without title acquires title to the object after having made the disposition.

In the case provided in the preceding paragraph. if several incompatible dispositions have been made, only the earliest disposition is effective.

CHAPTER V

DATES AND PERIODS

Article 119.—Unless otherwise provided, the calculation of dates and periods specified in law, ordinances, judicial decisions and juristic acts shall be made in accordance with the provisions of the present chapter.

Article 120.—A period fixed by hours shall commence immediately.

When a period is fixed by days, weeks, months or years, the first day is not included in the calculation.

Article 121.—A period fixed by days, weeks, months or years ends with the expiration of the last day of the period.

If a period fixed by weeks, months or years does not run from the beginning of a week, month or year, it ends with the expiration of the day preceding the day of the last week, month or year which corresponds to that on which it began to run. But if a period is fixed by months or years and there is no corresponding day in the last month, the period ends with the expiration of the last day of the last month.

Article 122.—If on a given date, or within a given period a declaration of intention is required to be made or an act of performance is to be effected, and if the given day or the last day of the given period, falls on a Sunday,

Chapter V *Dates and Periods*

THE CHINESE CIVIL CODE

Commemoration day or any other holiday, the day following the holiday shall take its place.

Article 123.—A period fixed by months or years is to be calculated according to the official calendar.

If a period of time is fixed by months or years in such a manner that they need not run consecutively, a month is reckoned as thirty days, a year as three hundred and sixty-five days.

Article 124.—Age is reckoned from the day of birth.

If it is not possible to ascertain the month and day of birth of a person, he is presumed to have been born on the first day of July. If the month of birth is known and it is not possible to ascertain the day, he is presumed to have been born on the fifteenth day of the month.

CHAPTER VI

EXTINCTIVE PRESCRIPTION

Article 125.—A right of claim is extinguished by prescription if not exercised within fifteen years, unless shorter periods are prescribed by law.

Article 126.—For the payment of interest, dividends, rent, maintenance, pensions, and other periodical prestations falling due at stated intervals of one year or less, the right of claim for each successive payment is extinguished by prescription if not exercised within five years.

Article 127.—Rights of claim in respect of the following are extinguished by prescription if not exercised within two years:—

$1°$ Charges for lodging, food or seats, or for the price of articles for consumption, and for disbursements, made by inns, restaurants and places of amusement.

$2°$ Cost of transportation and the disbursements by carriers.

$3°$ Rent due to a person who carries on a business of letting movables.

$4°$ Fees, charges for medicine and remuneration of medical practitioners, druggists and nurses, and their disbursements.

Chapter VI

THE CHINESE CIVIL CODE

5° Remuneration of attorneys, public accountants and notaries and their disbursements.

6° Restoration of things received from the parties to an action by attorneys, public accountants and notaries.

7° Remuneration of technical experts and contractors including their disbursements.

8° Claims of merchants, manufacturers and those who practise industrial arts for the price of goods or products supplied.

Article 128.—Extinctive prescription begins to run from the time when the claim can be exercised. If the claim is for a forbearance, the prescription begins to run from the moment when the right is first infringed.

Article 129.—Extinctive prescription is interrupted by and of the following causes:—

1. A demand (for the satisfaction of the claim);

2. An acknowledgment (of the claim);

3. An action (brought for the satisfaction of the claim).

The following are equivalent to bringing an action:

1. The service of an order for payment in a hortatory process;

2. The service of a summons for the purpose of effecting a compromise;

3. The presentation of a claim in bankruptcy proceedings;

4. The notice of the pendency of an action;

5. The institution of proceedings in execution or the presentation of an application for compulsory execution.

Extinctive Prescription

ARTICLES 128 TO 136

Article 130.—In the case of interruption by the making of a demand, if within six months an action in Court has not been brought for the satisfaction of the claim, the prescription is deemed not to have been interrupted.

Article 131.—In the case of interruption by bringing action, if the action is withdrawn or dismissed as nonconformable to law by a judgment which has become final, the prescription is deemed not to have been interrupted.

Article 132.—In the case of interruption by service of an order for payment, if the pendency of the action loses its effect, the prescription is deemed not to have been interrupted.

Article 133.—In the case of interruption by service of a summons for the purpose of effecting a compromise, if the other party does not appear or if no compromise is arrived at, the prescription is deemed not to have been interrupted.

Article 134.—In the case of interruption by presentation of a petition in bankruptcy proceedings, if the creditor withdraws the petition, the prescription is deemed not to have been interrupted.

Article 135.—In the case of interruption by notice of the pendency of an action, if no action is brought within six months after termination of the process, the prescription is deemed not to have been interrupted.

Article 136.—In the case of interruption by institution of proceedings in execution, if the order for execution is cancelled upon the application of the person entitled,

Chapter VI

THE CHINESE CIVIL CODE

or on account of the non-fulfilment of legal requirements, the prescription is deemed not to have been interrupted.

In the case of interruption by presentation of an application for compulsory execution, if the application is withdrawn or dismissed, the prescription is deemed not to have been interrupted.

Article 137.—A prescription which has been interrupted recommences to run from the moment when the cause of interruption ceases.

A prescription which has been interrupted by an action brought for the satisfaction of the claim recommences to run from the time when the case is decided or otherwise disposed of without any right of appeal.

Article 138.—An interruption of prescription takes effect only as between the parties and their successors and assignees.

Article 139.—If, at the time when the period for prescription would otherwise mature, the prescription cannot be interrupted owing to *force majeure* or any other unavoidable cause, the prescription is not complete before the expiration of one month from the time when such obstruction ceases.

Article 140.—The prescription of a claim in favour of or against the property of a succession is not complete before the expiration of six months from the time when the heir is determined, an administrator is appointed or a declaration of bankruptcy is made.

Article 141.—If a person incapable of disposing or limited in disposing capacity is left without a statutory

Extinctive Prescription

ARTICLES 137 TO 145

agent within six months before the expiration of the period of prescription, the prescription running against him is not complete before the expiration of six months from the time when such person becomes capable of disposing or when his statutory agent enters upon his duties.

Article 142.—The prescription of claims of a person incapable of disposing or limited in disposing capacity against his statutory agent is not complete before the expiration of one year after his legal relation to the statutory agent has ceased.

Article 143.—The prescription of claims of a husband against his wife or of a wife against her husband is not complete before the expiration of one year after the dissolution of marriage.

Article 144.—After the lapse of prescription the debtor is entitled to refuse performance.

If any prestation is made in satisfaction of a claim extinguished by prescription, the debtor cannot demand the return of the prestation on the ground that he was ignorant of the prescription. The same rule applies to a contractual acknowledgment of liability and to the giving of security.

Article 145.—The prescription of a claim for which there is a mortgage, or a right of pledge, or a right of retention does not prevent the creditor from satisfying himself out of the things mortgaged, pledged or retained.

The provision of the preceding paragraph does not apply to the claim for interest or other successive payments

Chapter VI   *Extinctive Prescription*

THE CHINESE CIVIL CODE

of periodical prestations when such claim has been extinguished by prescription.

Article 146.—Unless otherwise provided by law the effects of prescription of the principal extends to the accessory claims.

Article 147.—The period of prescription cannot be extended or reduced by juristic acts. The benefit of prescription cannot be renounced beforehand.

CHAPTER VII

EXERCISE OF RIGHTS

Article 148.—A right cannot be exercised for the main purpose of causing injury to another person.

Article 149.—A person acting for the purpose of defending his own rights or the rights of another person against any imminent unlawful infringement, is not liable to make compensation, provided that if anything is done in excess of what is required for necessary defence, a reasonable compensation is due.

Article 150.—A person acting for the purpose of averting an imminent danger threatening the body, liberty or property of himself or of another person, is not liable to make compensation, provided that the act is necessary for averting the danger and does not exceed the limit of the damage which would have been caused by the danger.

In the case provided in the preceding paragraph if the person so acting is responsible for the happening of the danger, he is liable to make compensation.

Article 151.—A person who, in order to protect his rights, exercises constraint over the liberty, or seizes or destroys the property, of another person, is not liable to make compensation, provided that the assistance of the authorities could not be obtained in due time and there

Chapter VII   *Exercise of Rights*

THE CHINESE CIVIL CODE

was a danger that if the person did not act immediately, the exercise of his right would be rendered impossible or obviously difficult.

Article 152.—A person who in conformity with the provisions of the preceding article restrains the liberty of another person or seizes his property must apply without delay for assistance from the authorities.

If such application is rejected or is not made in due time, he is liable to make compensation for any injury resulting from his action.

Book II

OBLIGATIONS

CHAPTER I

_____

GENERAL PROVISIONS

TITLE I.—SOURCES OF OBLIGATIONS

Part 1.—Contracts

Article 153.—A contract is concluded when the parties have reciprocally declared either expressly or tacitly their concording intention.

If the parties agree on all the essential elements of the contract but have expressed no intention as to the non-essential points, the contract is deemed to be concluded. In respect to the above mentioned non-essential points in the absence of an agreement, the Court shall decide them according to the nature of the affair.

Article 154.—A person who offers to make a contract is bound by his offer unless at the time of offer he excludes this obligation or unless it may be presumed from the circumstances or from the nature of the affair that he did not intend to be bound.

Exposing goods for sale with their selling price is deemed to be an offer. However, the sending of price-lists is not deemed to be an offer.

Article 155.—An offer ceases to be binding if it is refused.

Chapter I   *General Provisions*

The Chinese Civil Code

Article 156.—An offer made *inter presentes* ceases to be binding if not accepted at once.*

Article 157.—An offer made *inter absentes* ceases to be binding if not accepted by the other party within the time during which notice of acceptance may be expected to arrive under ordinary circumstances.

Article 158.—If a period of time for the acceptance of the offer has been fixed, the offer ceases to be binding if not accepted within such period.

Article 159.—If an acceptance arrives out of time though it has been sent in such a manner that under ordinary circumstances it ought to have arrived in due time, the offerer must immediately notify the acceptor of such delay.

If the offerer delays the sending of the notice specified in the foregoing paragraph, the acceptance is deemed to have arrived in due time.

Article 160.—An acceptance which arrives out of time is deemed to be a new offer.

An acceptance with amplifications, limitations or other alterations is deemed to be a refusal of the original offer coupled with the making of a new offer.

Article 161.—In cases where according to custom or owing to the nature of the affair, notification of acceptance is not necessary, the contract is concluded when, within a reasonable time, something has been done, which may be considered as an acceptance of the offer.

---

* *See* translator's note on Article 94.

Title I   *Sources of Obligations*

ARTICLES 156 TO 165

The provision of the foregoing paragraph applies *mutatis mutandis* when at the time of offer the offerer has waived notice of acceptance.

Article 162.—If a notification revoking an offer arrives after the arrival of the offer itself, though it has been sent in such a manner that under ordinary circumstances it ought to have arrived before or simultaneously with the arrival of the offer, the other party so notified must notify the promisor (offerer) immediately of such delay.

If such other party (the offeree) delays the sending of the notice specified in the preceding paragraph, the notification revoking the offer is deemed to have arrived with no delay.

Article 163.—The provisions of the preceding article apply *mutatis mutandis* to the revocation of acceptance.

Article 164.—When a person by public notice promises to reward another person for the performance of an act, he is bound to deliver the reward to the person who has performed the act. The same rule applies in respect to the person, who has performed such act without knowledge of the notice.

When the act specified in the preceding paragraph has been simultaneously or successively performed by several persons, if the promisor has delivered the reward to the person who has first notified the promisor of his performance, the obligation to deliver the reward is extinguished.

Article 165.—When a promise of reward made by

Chapter I   *General Provisions*

The Chinese Civil Code

public notice is revoked before the act is performed, the promisor is bound to compensate the person performing the act in good faith for damages arising therefrom, unless he can prove that that person would have never performed the act, but he is bound only up to the amount of the promised reward.

Article 166.—If it is agreed between the parties that a contract shall be executed in a certain definite form, the contract is presumed to be not concluded until executed in such form.

Part 2.—Conferring of Authority of Agency

Article 167.—If an authority of agency is conferred by a juristic act, the act of conferring shall be made by a declaration of intention to the agent or to the third party with whom the business delegated is transacted.

Article 168.—If several persons have been designated as agents, the business delegated must be transacted by them in common, except when it is otherwise provided by law or by a declaration of intention of the principal.

Article 169.—A person, who by his own acts represents that he has conferred the authority of agency to another person, or who knowing that another person declares himself to be his agent fails to express a contrary intention, is liable to third parties in the same way as a person who confers that authority, unless the third parties knew, or ought to have known, of the absence of authority.

Title I   *Sources of Obligations*

ARTICLES 166 TO 173

Article 170.—A juristic act done by a person having no authority to act as an agent is ineffective against the principal unless ratified by the principal.

In the case specified in the preceding paragraph, the other party to the juristic act may fix a reasonable period and request the principal to declare definitely within such period whether he ratifies or not. If the principal does not give a definite answer within the specified period, the ratification is deemed to have been refused.

Article 171.—A juristic act done by a person without authority may be revoked by the other party to the act before the ratification of the principal, except where such other party knew of the absence of authority at the time of the act.

Part 3.—Management of Affairs
Without Mandate

Article 172.—A person who takes charge of an affair of another person without having received a mandate from him nor having obligation to do so, shall manage the affair in conformity with the principal's expressed or presumptive wishes and in the manner which serves best the interest of the principal.

Article 173.—The manager must notify the principal without delay at the beginning of the management in so far as notification is possible. If there are no urgent circumstances, he must wait for the instructions of the principal.

| Chapter I | General Provisions |

THE CHINESE CIVIL CODE

The provisions of Articles 540 to 542 concerning Mandate apply *mutatis mutandis* to Management of Affairs Without Mandate.

Article 174.—If the undertaking of the management of the affair is opposed to the expressed or presumptive wishes of the principal, the manager is bound to compensate the principal for any injury arising from his management of the affair, even if no fault is imputable to him.

The provision of the preceding paragraph does not apply if the management of the affair is undertaken in order to fulfil an obligation of the principal which is of public interest or to fulfil a statutory duty of the principal to furnish maintenance to others.

Article 175.—If the undertaking of the management of the affair has for its object the averting of an imminent danger which threatens the life, body or property of the principal, the manager is responsible only in case of bad faith or gross negligence.

Article 176.—If the management of the affair is to the interest of the principal and is not contrary to his expressed or presumptive wishes, and where the manager has, for the principal, made necessary or beneficial expenses, or assumed debt, or suffered injury, he is entitled to claim from the principal the reimbursement of such expenses plus interest commencing from the date of outlay, or the payment of such debt, or compensation for the injury sustained.

In the cases provided for by paragraph 2 of Article 174

Title I   *Sources of Obligations*

ARTICLES 174 TO 180

this claim belongs to the manager, even if the undertaking of the management of the affair is opposed to the wishes of the principal.

Article 177.—If the management of the affair is contrary to the provisions of the preceding article, the principal is still entitled to the benefits acquired through the management. But the principal is bound towards the manager for the obligations specified in the first paragraph of the preceding article only to the extent of the benefits he acquired.

Article 178.—If the management of the affair is ratified by the principal, the provisions concerning Mandate shall apply.

Part 4.—Undue Enrichment

Article 179.—A person who without legal grounds acquires an advantage to the prejudice of another is bound to return it. The same rule applies if a legal ground originally existing disappears subsequently.

Article 180.—In any of the following cases, the prestation is not to be returned:—

1. if the prestation was made for the execution of a moral obligation;
2. if the prestation was made by the debtor for the execution of an obligation which was not yet due;
3. if the person who has made a prestation for the purpose of executing an obligation knew, at the time of performance, that he was not bound to execute;

Chapter I   *General Provisions*

THE CHINESE CIVIL CODE

4. if the prestation was made for an unlawful cause. However, this does not apply when the unlawful cause exists only with regard to the recipient.

Article 181.—In addition to the benefit received, a recipient unduly enriched must return whatever he acquired by virtue of such benefit. If restitution is impossible by reason of the very nature of the prestation or by reason of any other circumstance, he is bound to make good the value.

Article 182.—The recipient, who did not know of the absence of the legal ground and is no longer benefited, is released from the obligation to return or make good the value.

If the recipient knew of the absence of legal ground at the time of the receipt, or if he subsequently becomes aware of it, he is bound to return the advantages acquired at the time of the receipt of the prestation or such part of these advantages as still existed at the time when he became aware of the absence of the legal ground together with the interest, and to make compensation for the injury suffered, if any.

Article 183.—When the recipient unduly enriched transfers gratuitously whatever he receives to a third person, in consequence of which the recipient is released from his obligation to return the benefit, such third person is bound to make restitution to the extent to which the recipient is released from his obligation.

Title I   *Sources of Obligations*

Articles 181 to 187

Part 5.—*Wrongful Acts*

Article 184.—A person who, intentionally or by his own fault, wrongfully injures the rights of another is bound to compensate him for any damage arising therefrom. The same rule applies when the injury is done intentionally in a manner contrary to the rules of good morals.

A person who infringes a statutory provision enacted for the protection of others is presumed to have committed a fault.

Article 185.—If several persons have caused an injury to the right of another person by a wrongful act committed in common, they are jointly liable for the damage. The same rule applies if it cannot be discovered which of several participants has caused the damage.

Instigators and accomplices are deemed to be joint-doers.

Article 186.—An official who injures the rights of a third party by intentionally committing a breach of a duty which he ought to exercise in favour of such third party, is liable for any damage arising therefrom.   If the breach is the result of a fault of the official, he may be held liable only in so far as the injured party is unable to obtain compensation by other means.

In the case mentioned in the foregoing paragraph, the official is not liable, if the injured party has intentionally or by his own fault omitted to obviate the injury by making use of a legal remedy.

Article 187.—A person without disposing capacity or limited in disposing capacity, who has wrongfully

Chapter I   *General Provisions*

THE CHINESE CIVIL CODE

injured the rights of another, shall be liable jointly with his statutory representative for any damages arising therefrom if he is capable of discernment at the time of committing such act. If he is incapable of discernment at the time of committing the act, his statutory agent alone shall be liable for such damages.

In the case of the preceding paragraph, the statutory agent is not liable if he has committed no fault in his duty of supervision, or if the damage would have been occasioned notwithstanding the exercise of reasonable supervision.

If compensation cannot be obtained according to the provisions of the two preceding paragraphs, the Court may, on the application of the injured party, take into consideration the financial conditions of the doer and the injured party, and order the doer to compensate for a part or the whole of the damages.

The provisions of the preceding paragraph apply *mutatis mutandis* to cases where damage has been caused to a third party by a person in a condition of absence of discernment or of mental disorder other than those specified in the first paragraph.

Article 188.—The employer is jointly liable to make compensation for any damage which the employee wrongfully causes to the rights of another person in the performance of his duties. However, the employer is not liable for the damages if he has exercised reasonable care in the selection of the employee, and in the superintendence of the duties, or if the damage would have been occasioned notwithstanding the exercise of such reasonable care.

If compensation cannot be obtained by the injured

Title I   *Sources of Obligations*

ARTICLES 188 TO 191

party according to the proviso of the preceding paragraph, the Court may, on his application, taking into consideration the financial conditions of the employer and the injured party, order the employer to compensate for a part or the whole of the damages.

The employer who has made compensation as specified in the preceding paragraph has a right of recourse against the employee who has committed the wrongful act.

Article 189.—The employer is not liable for the damages wrongfully caused by a contractor to the rights of another person in the course of his work, unless the employer was at fault in regard to the work ordered or his instructions.

Article 190.—If damage is caused by an animal, the possessor is bound to compensate the injured party for any damage arising therefrom, unless he has exercised reasonable care in keeping it according to its species and nature, or unless the damage would have been occasioned notwithstanding the exercise of such reasonable care.

The possessor may exercise a right of recourse against the third person, who has excited or provoked the animal, or against the possessor of another animal which has caused the excitement or provocation.

Article 191.—If damage is caused by reason of defective construction or insufficient maintenance of a building or other work on land, the owner of such building or work is bound to make compensation, unless he has used reasonable care to prevent such happening that has caused the damage.

| Chapter I | General Provisions |

THE CHINESE CIVIL CODE

If, in the case of the foregoing paragraph, there is also some other person who is responsible for the cause of the damage, the owner making compensation may exercise a right of recourse against such person.

Article 192.—A person who wrongfully caused the death of another is also bound to make compensation for damages to any person incurring the funeral expenses.

If the victim was statutorily bound to furnish maintenance to a third party, the author of the act shall also make compensation to such third party for any damage arising therefrom.

Article 193.—If, in consequence of a wrongful injury to the body or health of another, his earning capacity is lost or decreased, or an increase of his necessities arises, the author of the injury is bound to make compensation to the injured party for any damage arising therefrom.

The Court may, on the application of the parties, order the aforesaid compensation to be made in periodical payments of money, but the Court must compel the author of the injury to furnish security.

Article 194.—In case of death caused by a wrongful act the father, mother, sons, daughters and spouse of the deceased may claim for a reasonable compensation in money for such damage as is not a purely pecuniary loss.

Article 195.—In the case of injury to the body, health, reputation or liberty of another, the injured party may claim a reasonable compensation in money for such damage as is not a purely pecuniary loss. If reputation

Title I   *Sources of Obligations*

ARTICLES 192 TO 198

has been injured, the injured party may also claim the taking of proper measures for the rehabilitation of his reputation.

The claim aforementioned cannot be transferred or inherited, except in the case of a claim for money compensation which has been acknowedged by contract or upon which an action has been commenced.

Article 196.—A person who has wrongfully injured a thing belonging to another is bound to make compensation to the injured party for the diminution of the value of the thing.

Article 197.—The claim for damages arising from a wrongful act is extinguished by prescription, if not exercised within two years from the time when the injury and the person bound to make compensation became known to the injured party. The same rule applies if ten years have elapsed from the date when the wrongful act was committed.

A person bound to make compensation must, even after the completion of prescription under the preceding paragraph, return to the injured party in accordance with the provisions concerning Undue Enrichment whatever he has acquired through a wrongful act to the prejudice of the injured party.

Article 198.—If a person acquires by a wrongful act a claim against the injured party, the latter may refuse performance even if the claim for avoidance of the claim is extinguished by prescription.

Chapter I   *General Provisions*

THE CHINESE CIVIL CODE

TITLE II.—OBJECT OF OBLIGATIONS

Article 199.—By virtue of an obligation the creditor is entitled to claim a prestation from the debtor.

A prestation may consist in something which cannot be valued in money.

A prestation may consist in a forbearance.

Article 200.—When the object of the prestation is determined only in kind, if its quality cannot be determined by the nature of the juristic act or the intention of the parties, the debtor must deliver a thing of medium quality.

In the case of the preceding paragraph if the debtor has done whatever is necessary for the delivery of such a thing, or if, with the consent of the creditor, he has designated a thing to be delivered, such thing is considered as the object of the prestation.

Article 201.—When the object of the obligation is a prestation of a particular kind of currency in vogue and when at the time of payment this currency is no longer in vogue, the debtor must make payment in another currency in vogue.

Article 202.—When the object of the prestation is expressed in a foreign currency in vogue, the debtor may make payment in Chinese currency at the market rate of the place and time of payment, unless it has been agreed upon by the parties that payment must be made in the foreign currency in vogue.

Article 203.—In the case of a debt bearing interest,

Title II   *Object of Obligations*

ARTICLES 199 TO 209

if no rate has been fixed by contract or by law, the rate shall be five per cent. (5%) per annum.

Article 204.—If the agreed rate of interest is over twelve per cent. (12%) per annum, the debtor may at any time after one year has elapsed repay the capital, but he must give to the creditor one month's previous notice.

The right of reimbursement specified in the preceding paragraph may not be excluded or limited by contract.

Article 205.—If the rate of interest agreed upon exceeds twenty per cent. (20%) per annum, the creditor is not entitled to claim any interest over and above twenty per cent. (20%).

Article 206.—The creditor cannot cunningly obtain any profit by discounting or by any other way in excess of the rate of interest specified in the preceding article.

Article 207.—Interest cannot be added to capital and again bear interest; however, if the parties have agreed upon in writing that the creditor may add to the capital the interest which has been in arrears for more than one year but has not been paid notwithstanding the demand of the creditor, such agreement shall be adhered to.

The provisions of the preceding paragraph do not apply in case there is a different trade custom.

Article 208.—When the prestation is to be selected from among several prestations, the right of choice belongs to the debtor, unless otherwise provided by law or by contract.

Article 209.—The debtor or creditor who has the

Chapter I	General Provisions

THE CHINESE CIVIL CODE

right of choice shall exercise it by a declaration of intention made to the other party.

If a third person has the right of choice, he shall exercise it by a declaration of intention made to the debtor and to the creditor.

Article 210.—If the choice is to be made within a fixed period of time and the party who has the right of choice does not exercise it within such period, the right of choice passes to the other party.

If no period of time is fixed, the party who has not the right of choice can, when the obligation becomes due, fix a reasonable time and notify the other party to exercise his right of choice within such time; if such party does not exercise his right of choice during the fixed time, the right of choice passes to the party who notifies.

If the choice is to be made by a third person and such person is unable or unwilling to make it, the right of choice passes to the debtor.

Article 211.—If one of the prestations is impossible from the beginning or becomes impossible subsequently, the obligation exists only in the prestations which remain possible, unless the impossibility arises through circumstances for which the party who has not the right of choice is responsible.

Article 212.—The effect of the choice is retroactive as from the time when the obligation was formed.

Article 213.—Unless otherwise provided by law or by contract, a person who is bound to make compensation for an injury must cause the injured party to be restored

Title II   *Object of Obligations*

ARTICLES 210 TO 217

to the condition which existed prior to the happening of the injury.

If the restoration of the prior condition consists in the payment of money, interest is due from the time the injury took place.

Article 214.—If the person who is under an obligation to restore the prior condition does not perform his obligation within a reasonable time fixed by the injured party, the latter can claim payment of damages for the injury sustained.

Article 215.—If the obligation to restore the prior condition cannot be performed, or if its performance is obviously hindered by great difficulties, payment of damages in money is due for the injury sustained.

Article 216.—Unless otherwise provided by law or by contract, damages shall be only for the injury actually suffered and for the profit which has been lost.

Profit is deemed to have been lost which could have been normally expected, either according to the ordinary course of things, or according to the projects or preparations made, or according to other special circumstances.

Article 217.—If the injured party has by his own fault contributed in causing or aggravating the injury, the Court may reduce the amount of damages or give no damages at all.

The injured party is deemed to have committed a fault if he has omitted to call beforehand the attention of the other party to danger of serious injury which the other party had not the means of knowing,

Chapter I *General Provisions*

THE CHINESE CIVIL CODE

or if he has omitted to avert or mitigate the injury.

Article 218.—When the injury was not caused intentionally or through gross negligence, if its reparation would seriously affect the means of livelihood of the person responsible for it, the Court may reduce the amount of damages.

Title III *Effects of Obligations*

ARTICLES 218 TO 224

TITLE III.—EFFECTS OF OBLIGATIONS

Part 1.—Performance

Article 219.—Every person is bound to execute his obligations and to exercise his rights in accordance with the rules of honesty and good faith.

Article 220.—The debtor is responsible for his acts, whether intentional or due to his fault.

The extent of responsibility for one's fault varies with the particular nature of the affair; but such responsibility shall be lessened, if the affair is not intended to procure an advantage to the debtor.

Article 221.—Where the debtor is a person without disposing capacity or limited in disposing capacity, his responsibility shall be determined according to the provisions of Article 187.

Article 222.—Liability for intentional acts or gross negligence cannot be released in advance.

Article 223.—A person who is answerable for such care as he is accustomed to exercise in the management of his own affairs, is responsible only for his gross negligence.

Article 224.—Unless otherwise agreed upon by the parties, a debtor is responsible for the intentional acts or fault of his agent and of the persons whom he employs in performing his obligation to the same extent as he is responsible for his own intentional acts or fault.

Chapter I   *General Provisions*

The Chinese Civil Code

Article 225.—The debtor is relieved from his obligation to perform if performance becomes impossible by reason of a circumstance for which he is not responsible.

If, in consequence of the impossibility of performance under the preceding paragraph, the debtor is entitled to claim for damages against a third party, the creditor may demand from the debtor the transfer of the claim for damages, or the delivery of the compensation he has received.

Article 226.—If performance becomes impossible by reason of a circumstance for which the debtor is responsible, the creditor may demand compensation for any injury resulting therefrom.

In the case provided for in the preceding paragraph, if part of the performance is impossible and the remaining part, if performed, will be of no advantage to the creditor, the creditor may refuse it and demand compensation for the non-performance of the entire obligation.

Article 227.—If a debtor fails to perform his obligation, or performs it only in part, the creditor may apply to the Court for compulsory execution and claim for damages.

Article 228.—A person bound to made compensation for the loss of or injury to a thing or right may demand from another, who is entitled to claim for damages, the transfer of the claims which the latter has against third parties by virtue of his ownership of the said thing, or by virtue of the said right.

Title III   *Effects of Obligations*

ARTICLES 225 TO 232

Part 2.—Default

Article 229.—When the time fixed for the performance of an obligation is definite, the debtor is in default from the moment when such time expires.

When no definite time has been fixed for the performance of the obligation and when the creditor is entitled to claim performance, but the debtor does not perform the same after notice has been given by the creditor, the debtor is in default from the moment when he has been notified. Instituting an action for performance, or the service of an order for payment according to hortatory process is equivalent to a notice.

If a time for performance is fixed in the notice aforementioned, the debtor is in default from the moment when such time expires.

Article 230.—The debtor is not in default if the prestation has not been effected by reason of circumstances for which he is not responsible.

Article 231.—When the debtor is in default, the creditor is entitled to claim compensation for any injury resulting therefrom.

So long as the default continues, the debtor aforementioned is also responsible for any injury resulting from circumstances of *force majeure,* unless he can prove that the injury would have been sustained, even if he had performed in due time.

Article 232.—If, after the default, the performance is of no more interest to the creditor, he can refuse the

| Chapter I | General Provisions |

THE CHINESE CIVIL CODE

performance and claim compensation for damages resulting from non-performance.

Article 233.—When the object of an obligation which is in default is money, the creditor can claim interest for the default, which is to be calculated at the legal rate. But if a higher rate of interest had been agreed upon, this higher rate shall apply.

Interest shall not be paid upon interest in default.

In cases specified in the preceding two paragraphs, the creditor can claim compensation for other injury, upon proof of same.

Article 234.—If the creditor refuses or fails to accept the performance tendered to him, he is in default from the moment when the performance is tendered.

Article 235.—If the debtor does not actually tender the performance according to the tenor of the obligation, the tender shall be ineffective. But if the creditor has previously declared that he will not accept performance, or if in order to effect the performance, an act of the creditor is necessary, the debtor may give notice to the creditor that he (the debtor) is ready to perform. In such a case, the notice by the debtor is equivalent to a tender.

Article 236.—If no definite time has been fixed for the performance, or if the debtor is entitled to perform before the fixed time, the creditor is not in default by the mere fact that he is temporarily prevented from accepting the tendered performance, unless the performance was tendered on a notice given by the creditor, or unless the debtor has notified the creditor a reasonable time beforehand.

Title III   *Effects of Obligations*

ARTICLES 233 TO 243

Article 237.—During the default of the creditor, the debtor is responsible only for his intentional acts or gross negligence.

Article 238.—The debtor is not liable to pay interest during the default of the creditor.

Article 239.—If the debtor has to return the fruits produced by an object or to make reimbursement for them, his liability during the default of the creditor is limited to the fruits which he actually collects.

Article 240.—In case of the default of the creditor, the debtor may demand compensation for the necessary expenses which he may have incurred for the tender, as well as for the preservation of the object of the prestation.

Article 241.—When the debtor is under an obligation to deliver an immovable property, he may, after the creditor is in default, abandon its possession.

In the case of abandonment under the preceding paragraph, the debtor is bound to notify the creditor in advance, unless such notification is impossible.

Part 3.—Preservation

Article 242.—The creditor may, in order to protect and satisfy his obligation, exercise in his own name any right of the debtor which the debtor neglects to exercise, except rights which are strictly personal to the debtor.

Article 243.—So long as the debtor is not in default, the creditor can not exercise the rights specified in the preceding article, except those rights which are exclusively for the preservation of the rights of the said debtor.

Chapter I   *General Provisions*

The Chinese Civil Code

Article 244.—If a gratuitous act done by the debtor is likely to be prejudicial to the rights of the creditor, the creditor may apply to the Court for the cancellation of such act.

If the debtor does a non-gratuitous act knowing at the time of the act that it is likely to be prejudicial to the rights of the creditor, the creditor may apply to the Court for the cancellation of such act, provided that the party who profited by the act also knew of the circumstances on the receipt of the benefits.

The provisions of the preceding two paragraphs do not apply to acts done by the debtor, the object of which is not property.

Article 245.—The right to claim cancellation in accordance with the provisions of the preceding article shall be extinguished by prescription if not exercised within one year from the moment when the creditor knew of the grounds for cancellation, or shall be extinguished after ten years from the date of the act.

Part 4.—Contracts

Article 246.—A contract for an impossible prestation is void. However, if the impossibility can be removed and if the parties, at the time when the contract was concluded, intended to have it performed after the removal of the impossibility, the contract is valid.

If the contract is subject to a condition precedent or to a time of commencement, and the impossibility is removed prior to the happening of the condition or prior to the time, the contract is valid.

Title III   *Effects of Obligations*

ARTICLES 244 TO 249

Article 247.—When a contract is void on account of impossibility of performance, the party who at the time of contract knew or had the means of knowing the impossibility is liable for the injury caused to the other party who, without fault of his own, believed in the validity of the contract.

The provision of the preceding paragraph applies *mutatis mutandis,* if the prestation is partially impossible and the contract is valid in respect to the possible part, or if one of several prestations subject to a choice is impossible.

Article 248.—When one of the parties to a contract receives earnest money from the other, the contract is deemed to be concluded.

Article 249.—Unless otherwise agreed upon by the parties, the following rules apply to earnest money:—

1.   On the contract being performed, earnest money shall be returned or treated as part payment.

2.   If the contract cannot be performed owing to a circumstance for which the party who gave the earnest money is responsible, such party shall not claim for the return of the earnest money.

3.   If the contract cannot be performed owing to a circumstance for which the party who received the earnest money is responsible, such party shall return double the amount of the earnest money.

4.   If the contract cannot be performed owing to a circumstance for which neither of the parties is responsible, the earnest money shall be returned.

| *Chapter I* | *General Provisions* |

The Chinese Civil Code

Article 250.—The parties may agree on a penalty to be paid by the debtor in case the debtor does not perform the obligation.

Unless otherwise agreed upon by the parties, the penalty shall be deemed to be the total amount of damages due for non-performance. But if it is agreed that the penalty is only for non-performance of the obligation at the agreed time or in the agreed way, the creditor may, if the obligation is not performed, claim performance or damages for non-performance, in addition to penalty.

Article 251.—If there has been part performance, the Court may reduce the penalty proportionately as the creditor has been benefited by the part performance.

Article 252.—If the stipulated penalty is disproportionately high, the Court may reduce it to a reasonable amount.

Article 253.—The provisions of the three preceding articles apply *mutatis mutandis* where the stipulated penalty is for a prestation other than money.

Article 254.—When a party to a contract is in default, the other party may fix a reasonable time and notify him to perform within that time. If he does not perform within that time, the other party may rescind the contract.

Article 255.—If according to the nature of the contract or the intention of the parties, the object of the contract can be accomplished only by performance at a fixed time, which said time elapses without one of the parties having performed, the other party may rescind

Title III   *Effects of Obligations*

ARTICLES 250 TO 259

the contract without giving the notification specified in the preceding article.

Article 256.—In cases provided by Article 226, the creditor may rescind the contract.

Article 257.—If no time is fixed for the exercise of the right of rescission the other party may fix a reasonable period and notify the party having the right of rescission to make a definite reply within such period whether he will rescind or not. If notice of rescission is not received within such period, the right of rescission is extinguished.

Article 258.—Rescission is effected by a declaration of intention made to the other party.

If there are in the contract several persons on either side the declaration of intention to rescind specified in the preceding paragraph must be made by all or to all.

A declaration of intention for the rescission of a contract cannot be revoked.

.*Article* 259.—Unless otherwise provided for by law or by contract, each party must, in case of rescission, restore the other party to his former condition, observing the following rules:—

1. Each party must restore to the other party the prestation received.

2. If the prestation received consisted of money, interest is to be added, calculated from the time when the money was received.

3. If the prestation received consisted in services or in the use of a thing, the value of such services or use at the time when the prestation was received must be reimbursed in money.

Chapter I   *General Provisions*

THE CHINESE CIVIL CODE

4. If a thing to be restored has produced fruits, such fruits shall be restored.

5. If for a thing to be restored, necessary or beneficial expenses have been made, the reimbursement of such expenses may be claimed for to the extent to which the other party was still benefited at the time of the restoration.

6. If a thing to be restored has been destroyed or damaged or cannot be restored owing to any other cause, its value must be reimbursed.

Article 260.—The exercise of the right of rescission does not prejudice the right to claim for damages.

Article 261.—The provisions of Articles 264 to 267 apply *mutatis mutandis,* when the obligations of the parties resulting from the rescission are mutual.

Article 262.—When the person entitled to rescission has, through causes for which he is responsible, damaged or destroyed the thing received, or, when any other circumstance makes restoration thereof impossible, his right of rescission is extinguished. The same rule applies when the nature of the thing received has been altered by working it up or remodelling it.

Article 263.—The provisions of Articles 258 and 260 apply *mutatis mutandis* when the parties terminate the contract in accordance with the provisions of law.

Article 264.—A party to a mutual contract may, unless he is bound to perform first, refuse to perform his part, until the counter-prestation has been performed by the other party.

When one party has partially performed his part,

Title III   *Effects of Obligations*

ARTICLES 260 TO 268

counter-performance cannot be refused, if circumstances are such that a refusal to perform would constitute a breach of honesty and good faith.

Article 265.—A person who is bound to perform his part first may, if after the conclusion of the contract the financial circumstances of the other party have obviously decreased whereby counter-performance is feared to be difficult, refuse to perform his obligation, until the other party has performed his part or given security for such performance.

Article 266.—If, through a cause for which none of the parties is responsible, performance by one of the parties has become wholly impossible, the other party is discharged from his obligation to perform the counter-prestation. If impossibility is only partial, the counter-prestation is reduced proportionately.

In the case provided for in the preceding paragraph, if the counter-prestation has been performed wholly or in part, the party who performed it may, in accordance with the provisions concerning Undue Enrichment, claim its restoration.

Article 267.—If one of the parties finds it impossible to perform his obligation through a cause for which the other party is responsible, the former may claim for the counter-prestation, but he must deduct from it what he might save or ought to have saved by being released from his own obligation.

Article 268.—One of the parties to a contract who has undertaken that a prestation shall be performed by

Chapter I   *General Provisions*

THE CHINESE CIVIL CODE

a third party is liable for damages if the third party does not perform the prestation.

Article 269.—When it is provided in a contract that an obligation shall be performed to a third person, the promisee may demand from the debtor that he performs the obligation to the third person, and such third person also has the right to demand performance direct from the debtor.

So long as the third person has not declared his intention to take advantage of the contract specified in the preceding paragraph, the parties may modify the contract or cancel it.

If the third person declares to one or the other of the parties his intention not to take advantage of the contract he is deemed never to have had any right under the contract.

Article 270.—The debtor specified in the preceding article may set up against the third person so benefited all the defences arising out of the contract.

Title IV   *Plurality of Creditors and Debtors*

ARTICLES 269 TO 275

TITLE IV.—PLURALITY OF CREDITORS AND DEBTORS

Article 271.—When several persons are together debtors or creditors of one and the same obligation, and the prestation is divisible, each of them is liable for, or entitled to, an equal share in the prestation, unless otherwise provided by law or by contract. The same rule applies when a prestation which was originally indivisible is converted into a divisible prestation.

Article 272.—A liability is said to be "joint" when several persons bound under one and the same obligation expressly declare that each of them is bound to the creditor for the whole of the prestation.

Failing the declaration specified in the preceding article, joint liability exists only in the cases specified by law.

Article 273.—The creditor of a joint obligation is entitled to demand total or partial performance from anyone of the debtors, or from several or all of them, simultaneously or successively.

All the debtors remain jointly bound to the creditor until the obligation has been performed in full.

Article 274.—If one of the joint debtors has extinguished the obligation by performance, prestation in lieu of performance, lodgment, set-off or merger, the other joint debtors are also discharged from the obligation.

Article 275.—A non-appellable judgment rendered in favour of one of the joint debtors and based on facts

Chapter I   *General Provisions*

THE CHINESE CIVIL CODE

which are not personal to such debtor, operates in favour of all the joint debtors.

Article 276.—When the creditor grants a release to one of the joint debtors without expressing his intention to extinguish the whole obligation, such release operates in favour of the other debtors only up to the amount of the share which is incumbent on such debtor.

When prescription has been completed as regards one of the joint debtors, the provisions of the preceding paragraph apply *mutatis mutandis.*

Article 277.—A claim belonging to one of the joint debtors against the creditor may be set off by any of the debtors, only up to the amount of the share which is incumbent on such debtor.

Article 278.—The default of the creditor towards one of the joint debtors operates also in favour of all the said debtors.

Article 279.—The consequences of facts other than those specified in the five preceding articles or other than those provided by contract, operate only in favour of or against the particular joint debtors to whom they refer.

Article 280.—The joint debtors as between themselves, unless otherwise provided by law or by contract, are liable for equal shares in the obligation. However, the costs and damages resulting from facts for which one of the joint debtors is personally liable are to be borne by him.

Article 281.—When one of the joint debtors has

Title IV   *Plurality of Creditors and Debtors*

ARTICLES 276 TO 284

secured the discharge of the other joint debtors by performing the obligation or by other acts, he is entitled to demand from the other debtors the reimbursement of their respective shares in the prestation, plus interest from the date of discharge.

In the case specified in the preceding paragraph, the debtor entitled to claim reimbursement is subrogated to the rights of the creditor to the amount of the reimbursement which the said debtor is entitled to demand, but such debtor cannot exercise them to the detriment of the creditor.

Article 282.—If one of the joint debtors cannot reimburse his share, the deficiency shall be borne *pro rata* by the other debtors, including the debtor entitled to claim reimbursement, but if the impossibility to reimburse is due to the fault of the latter, he cannot claim that the other debtors shall bear their shares.

In the case of the preceding paragraph, if one of those other debtors is discharged of his own share in the obligation, he is, however, in accordance with the provisions of the preceding paragraph, liable for his share in the deficiency.

Article 283.—A claim is said to be "joint," when several persons are entitled by law or by juristic act to the benefit of one and the same obligation in such a way that each creditor can demand the whole of the prestation from the debtor.

Article 284.—The debtor to a joint claim may at his option perform wholly in favour of any of the joint creditors.

| *Chapter I* | *General Provisions* |

THE CHINESE CIVIL CODE

Article 285.—A demand made by one of the joint creditors operates in favour of all the joint creditors.

Article 286.—If the obligation is extinguished on account of one of the creditors having been satisfied by performance, prestation in lieu of performance, lodgment, set-off or merger, the rights of the other creditors are also extinguished.

Article 287.—A non-appellable judgment rendered in favour of one of the joint creditors operates in favour of all the joint creditors.

A non-appellable judgment rendered against one of the joint creditors and based on facts which are not personal to such creditor operates against all the creditors.

Article 288.—A release granted to the debtor by one of the joint creditors operates against the other creditors only up to the amount of the share to which the creditor who granted the release is entitled.

When prescription has been completed against one of the joint creditors, the provisions of the preceding paragraph apply *mutatis mutandis*.

Article 289.—Default of one of the joint creditors operates against all the joint creditors.

Article 290.—The consequences of facts other than those specified in the five preceding articles or other than those provided by contract, operate only in favour of or against the particular joint creditors to whom they refer.

Article 291.—The joint creditors, as against themselves, unless otherwise provided by law or by contract, are entitled to equal shares of benefit in the obligation.

Title IV   *Plurality of Creditors and Debtors*

Articles 285 to 293

Article 292.—When several persons are joint debtors or creditors of one and the same obligation, and the prestation is indivisible, the provisions concerning joint debtors or joint creditors shall apply *mutatis mutandis,* reserving the provisions of Article 293.

Article 293.—In an indivisible prestation, the creditor may demand performance only on behalf of all the creditors; and the debtor may perform only in favour of all the creditors.

Except as provided for in the preceding paragraph, facts which affect the obligation between the debtor and one of the creditors do not operate in favour of or against the other creditors.

Chapter I *General Provisions*

The Chinese Civil Code

Title V.—Transfer of Obligations

Article 294.—A creditor may transfer a claim of an obligation to a third party, unless:

1. its nature does not permit of it;
2. the parties have agreed that the claim shall not be transferred; or
3. the claim is not subject to judicial attachment.

The agreement mentioned in the second section of the foregoing paragraph cannot be set up against a *bonâ fide* third person.

Article 295.—The transfer of a claim includes the transfer of all the securities and other rights accessory to it, but this does not apply to those rights which cannot be separated from the person of the transferor.

Interests in arrears are presumed to be included in the transfer of the capital.

Article 296.—The transferor is bound to deliver to the transferee all documents which serve as evidence of the claim, and to give him all informations necessary for the assertion of such claim.

Article 297.—The transfer of a claim is not effective as against the debtor until the debtor has been notified of it by the transferor or by the transferee, unless otherwise provided for by law.

Tender by the transferee to the debtor of the deed of transfer executed by the transferor is equivalent to notice.

Article 298.—When the transferor has notified the debtor that he has transferred the claim, the debtor may

Title V   *Transfer of Obligations*

ARTICLES 294 TO 302

set up against the transferor all the defences which he has against the transferee, even though the transfer is not executed or is invalid.

The notice under the preceding paragraph may be revoked only with the consent of the transferee.

Article 299.—The debtor can set up against the transferee all the defences which he had against the transferor at the time he received notice of the transfer.

The debtor can set off against the transferee any claim which he had against the transferor at the time he received notice of the transfer, provided such claim matures before the transferred claim, or simultaneously with it.

Article 300.—When a third person agrees with the creditor to assume the obligation of the debtor, the debt is transferred to the third person on the contract being concluded.

Article 301.—When a third person agrees with the debtor to assume the obligation of the debtor, the transfer is not effective as regards the creditor, unless he has agreed to it.

Article 302.—The debtor or the person assuming the debt under the preceding article may fix a reasonable period and notify the creditor to reply definitely within such period whether he agrees to the transfer or not. If the creditor does not give a definite reply within such period, he is deemed to have refused to agree to the said transfer.

If the creditor refuses to agree to the transfer, the

Chapter I   *General Provisions*

THE CHINESE CIVIL CODE

debtor or the person assuming the debt may rescind the contract.

Article 303.—The person assuming the debt can set up against the creditor all defences, which, on account of their legal relations, the debtor might have set up against the creditor. However, he cannot set off a claim belonging to the debtor.

The person assuming the debt cannot set up against the creditor any defences which, on account of the legal relations arising from the assumption of the debt, he might have set up against the debtor.

Article 304.—The assumption of a debt does not affect the existence of the accessory rights of the claim, unless the accessory rights are such that they cannot be separated from the person of the debtor.

The securities given by a third person for the performance of the obligation are extinguished by the assumption of the debt, unless such third person has agreed to the assumption.

Article 305.—In case of transfer of the assets and liabilities constituting the whole of the property or enterprise of a person, assumption of the debts becomes effective from the moment the transfer has been published or has been notified to the creditor.

In the case specified in the preceding paragraph, the original debtor remains jointly liable with the person assuming the debt for a period of two years from the date of notice or publication of the transfer for the obligations due, or from the date of maturity for the obligations which are not yet due.

Title V   *Transfer of Obligations*

ARTICLES 303 TO 306

Article 306.—The provisions of the preceding article relating to the transfer of the whole property also apply when several enterprises are amalgamated and their assets and liabilities are assumed by each other. In this case, the new enterprise resulting from the amalgamation becomes responsible for all the liabilities of the original enterprises.

Chapter I   *General Provisions*

THE CHINESE CIVIL CODE

TITLE VI.—EXTINCTION OF OBLIGATIONS

Part 1.—*General Provisions*

Article 307.—When the obligation is extinguished, the securities given for its performance, and other accessory rights are extinguished simultaneously.

Article 308.—On an obligation being wholly extinguished, the debtor may require the creditor to return or cancel the document in which the obligation is embodied. If the obligation has been only partly extinguished, or if the document entitles the creditor to other rights, the debtor may demand that particulars of the extinction be endorsed on the document.

If the creditor alleges that he cannot return or endorse the document, the debtor may require from the creditor a publicly certified acknowledgment showing that the obligation has been extinguished.

Part 2.—*Performance*

Article 309.—When performance has been made to the creditor or to his qualified representative in conformity with the tenor of the obligation, and accepted, the obligation is extinguished.

The bearer of a receipt signed by the creditor is deemed to be qualified to receive performance. But this rule does not apply, if the debtor knew, or, by reason of his own fault, was ignorant that the bearer was not qualified to receive performance.

Title VI   *Extinction of Obligations*

ARTICLES 307 TO 314

Article 310.—If performance is made to a third person and has been accepted by him, the following rules apply:—

1.   Performance is valid if the creditor ratifies it or if the third person subsequently acquires the obligation;

2.   Performance made to the quasi possessor of the claim is valid, if the person making performance did not know that the possessor is not a creditor;

3.   In cases other than those specified in the two preceding sections, performance is valid only to the extent to which the creditor has been enriched thereby.

Article 311.—An obligation may be performed by a third person except when the parties have otherwise agreed or when the nature of the obligation does not permit of it.

If the debtor objects to the obligation being performed by a third person, the creditor may refuse such performance, but this provision does not apply if it is to the advantage of the third person that the obligation be performed.

Article 312.—A third person who makes performance because it is to his advantage can exercise in his own name and up to the due amount all the rights which the creditor had in respect to the obligation, but he cannot enforce them to the detriment of the creditor.

Article 313.—The provisions of Articles 297 and 299 apply *mutatis mutandis* to the subrogation specified in the preceding article.

Article 314.—If the place of performance is not

Chapter I   *General Provisions*

THE CHINESE CIVIL CODE

fixed by law or by contract or by custom or cannot be inferred from the nature of the obligation or from other circumstances, the following rules shall apply:—

1. If the object of the obligation is to deliver a specific thing, performance shall be made at the place where such thing was at the time when the contract was concluded.

2. The other obligations shall be performed at the place of the creditor's domicile.

Article 315.—If the time of performance is not otherwise provided by law or by contract or cannot be inferred from the nature of the obligation or from other circumstances, the creditor may demand performance at any time and the debtor may also perform at any time.

Article 316.—If a time has been fixed for performance, the creditor may not demand performance before that time; but if no contrary intention has been expressed, the debtor may perform earlier.

Article 317.—Unless otherwise provided by law or by contract, the costs of performance shall be borne by the debtor. But if the creditor has increased the costs of performance by changing his domicile or by any other acts, the additional cost shall be borne by the creditor.

Article 318.—A debtor is not entitled to perform in part. However, the Court may, taking into consideration the position of the debtor, allow him to perform by instalments or to delay his performance in such reasonable time as may not greatly prejudice the interest of the creditor.

Title VI   Extinction of Obligations

ARTICLES 315 TO 322

In case the prestation is indivisible, the Court may, subject to the proviso of the preceding paragraph, allow the debtor to delay his performance.

Article 319.—If the creditor accepts in lieu of performance a prestation other than that originally agreed upon, the obligation is extinguished.

Article 320.—When the debtor, for the purpose of satisfying his creditor, has assumed a new obligation towards him, the original obligation revives, if the new obligation is not performed, unless a contrary intention has been expressed by the parties.

Article 321.—If a debtor is bound to the same creditor to make similar prestations in respect to several obligations, and if the prestation effected is insufficient for the discharge of all the obligations, the prestation goes towards discharging the obligations which the person performing specifies when effecting the prestation.

Article 322.—If the person performing has not made the specification provided in the preceding article, the following rules shall apply:—

1. The prestation must go first towards discharging such of the obligations which is due;

2. If several of the obligations are due or if none is due, the prestation must go first towards discharging the obligation which affords the creditor the least security; among several obligations equally secured, the prestation must go first towards discharging the one whose extinction is the most advantageous to the debtor; if there are several such obligations, the prestation must

Chapter I   General Provisions

THE CHINESE CIVIL CODE

go towards discharging the one which is maturing first;

3. If there are several obligations whose extinction is equally advantageous to the debtor and which are maturing at the same time, the prestation must be apportioned between them *pro rata*.

Article 323.—The prestation tendered by a person making performance shall go first towards discharging the expenses, then the interest and finally the capital. The same rule applies when an obligation is performed according to the provisions of the two preceding articles.

Article 324.—The person making performance may demand from the person accepting the performance the delivery of a written receipt.

Article 325.—In case of payment of interest or other periodical performance, if the creditor gives a receipt for one term without any reservation for the other terms, it is presumed that he has received performance for the previous terms.

If he gives a receipt for the capital, it is presumed that he has received the interest.

If the document embodying the obligation has been surrendered, it is presumed that the obligation has been extinguished.

Part 3.—Lodgment

Article 326.—When the creditor is in default, or when it is impossible to know exactly who is the creditor so that performance becomes difficult, the person entitled to perform may lodge the prestation for the creditor.

Title VI *Extinction of Obligations*

ARTICLES 323 TO 331

Article 327.—Lodgment must be made at the public lodgment office of the place of performance. If there is no such public office, the Court of the first degree of the place of performance shall, on the application of the person entitled to perform, designate a lodgment office or appoint a guardian over the thing lodged.

The person who makes lodgment must, after the lodgment has been made, notify the creditor immediately. If the person neglects to make such notification, he is bound to make compensation for all damage arising therefrom, unless notification was impossible.

Article 328.—After the thing is on lodgment, the creditor bears the risk of the thing being lost or damaged, and the debtor is not bound to pay interest nor to compensate for failure to collect fruits.

Article 329.—The creditor is entitled to take delivery of the thing lodged at any time. If, however, the debtor is bound to perform only after a counter-prestation has been effected by the creditor, the debtor may prevent the delivery of the thing lodged, until the counter-prestation is performed or proper security is given.

Article 330.—The right of the creditor to the thing lodged is extinguished by prescription, if not exercised within ten years from the day of lodgment; and in such a case, the ownership of the thing lodged passes to the Treasury.

Article 331.—If the object of the prestation is not suitable for lodgment or if it is feared that it would be lost or damaged or if its lodgment would involve

Chapter I   *General Provisions*

THE CHINESE CIVIL CODE

disproportionate expenses, the person entitled to perform may apply to the Court of the first degree of the place of performance to have it sold by auction and to lodge the proceeds of the sale.

Article 332.—When the object of the prestation mentioned in the preceding article has a current market value, the Court may allow the person entitled to perform to sell it at such market value and to lodge the proceeds of the sale.

Article 333.—The costs of lodgment, auction or sale, are to be borne by the creditor.

Part 4.—Set-Off

Article 334.—If two persons are bound to each other by obligations the objects of which are similar prestations and which are due, each party may be discharged from his own obligations by a set-off, unless the nature of the obligations does not permit of it.

Article 335.—The set-off is made by a declaration of intention by one party to the other. As between themselves, the obligations, in relating back to the moment at which there could first have been a set-off, are extinguished to the extent of the corresponding amounts of the obligations.

The declaration of intention specified in the preceding paragraph is ineffective, if made subject to a condition or to a time of commencement or ending.

Article 336.—A set-off may be made even though the obligations are to be performed in different places;

Title VI   Extinction of Obligations

ARTICLES 332 TO 343

but the party who declares the set-off must indemnify the other party for any injury resulting therefrom.

Article 337.—An obligation may also be set off even after the claim of it has been extinguished by prescription, provided that set-off was possible prior to its extinction.

Article 338.—The debtor of an obligation, which is not subject to a judicial attachment, cannot declare the said obligation extinguished by a set-off.

Article 339.—The debtor of an obligation resulting from an intentional wrongful act cannot declare the said obligation extinguished by a set-off.

Article 340.—When an obligation has been attached by an order of the Court, the third debtor of such obligation cannot set-off against it a claim which he has acquired from the creditor after the attachment.

Article 341.—When it is provided in a contract that an obligation shall be performed to a third person, the debtor of such obligation cannot set-off against it obligations which are due to him by the other party to the contract.

Article 342.—The provisions of Articles 321 to 323 apply *mutatis mutandis* to set-off.

Part 5.—Release

Article 343.—An obligation is extinguished if the creditor has declared to the debtor his intention to release the debtor from his obligation.

Chapter I

General Provisions

THE CHINESE CIVIL CODE

Part 6.—Merger

Article 344.—When the right and liability of an obligation become vested in the same person, the obligation is extinguished, except when it was the subject of a right of another person or when it is otherwise provided for by law.

Chapter II

PARTICULAR KINDS OF OBLIGATIONS

Title I.—Sale

Part 1.—General Provisions

Article 345.—A sale is a contract whereby the parties agree that one of them shall transfer to the other his rights over a property and the latter shall pay a price for it.

The contract of sale is completed when the parties have mutually agreed on the object to be sold and on the price to be paid.

Article 346.—Although the price is not fixed by the agreement, if it may be deducted from the circumstances, it is deemed to be fixed.

If it is agreed that the price shall be fixed according to the market price, it is deemed to be fixed according to such market price at the place and time of performance unless otherwise provided for by contract.

Article 347.—The provisions under the present title apply *mutatis mutandis* to such non-gratuitous contracts other than those of sale, unless the nature of the contract does not permit of it.

Chapter II   *Particular Kinds of Obligations*

THE CHINESE CIVIL CODE

Part 2.—Effects of Sale

Article 348.—The seller of a thing is bound to deliver it to the buyer and to cause him to acquire its ownership.

The seller of a right is bound to cause the buyer to acquire the right sold. If, by virtue of such right, the seller can possess a certain thing, he is also bound to deliver that thing.

Article 349.—The seller must warrant that the thing sold is free from any right enforceable by third parties against the buyer.

Article 350.—The seller of a claim or of any other right must warrant the actual existence of such claim or right. The seller of a valuable security must also warrant that it shall not be declared invalid through public summons.

Article 351.—If the buyer knew at the time of concluding the contract the defect of the right sold, the seller is not bound to warrant such defect, unless otherwise provided for by contract.

Article 352.—Unless otherwise provided for by contract, the seller of a claim does not warrant the solvency of the debtor.

If he warrants the solvency of the debtor he is presumed to warrant the solvency at the time when the claim is transferred.

Article 353.—If the seller does not perform his duties specified in Articles 348 to 351, the buyer can

Title I   *Sale*

ARTICLES 348 TO 356

exercise his rights in accordance with the provisions concerning non-performance of obligations.

Article 354.—The seller of a thing warrants that the thing sold is, at the time when the risk passes to the buyer according to the provisions of Article 373, free from any defect in quality which may impair or destroy its value, or its fitness for ordinary purposes, or its fitness for the purposes of the contract of sale. However, if the extent of the impairment is of no importance, such impairment cannot be deemed to be a defect.

The seller also warrants that, at the time the risk passes, the thing has the promised qualities.

Article 355.—A seller is not responsible for such defect of quality in the thing sold as specified in the first paragraph of the preceding article, if the buyer knew of the defect at the time when the contract was made.

If a defect of the kind specified in the first paragraph of the preceding article has remained unknown to the buyer in consequence of gross negligence, the seller is not responsible if he has not guaranteed that the thing is free from the defect, except in the case that he has intentionally concealed it.

Article 356. The buyer is bound to examine without delay the thing received by him in accordance with the nature of such thing and as far as the ordinary course of affairs allows it, and should he discover any defect for which the seller is responsible, he must immediately notify the seller of such defect.

| *Chapter II* | *Particular Kinds of Obligations* |

The Chinese Civil Code

If the buyer delays giving the notice mentioned in the preceding paragraph, he is deemed to have accepted the thing, except in case where the defect is one which would not have been revealed by ordinary examination.

Should a defect, which could not have been discovered immediately, be discovered subsequently, notice must be sent by the buyer without delay after the discovery. If he delays giving such notice, the thing is deemed to be accepted.

Article 357.—The provisions of the preceding article do not apply to cases where the seller has intentionally concealed the defect.

Article 358.—A buyer, who declines to accept a thing forwarded from another place by asserting that it is defective, is bound to preserve it in his custody temporarily, when the seller has no agent in the place of acceptance.

In the case specified in the preceding paragraph, if the buyer fails to take proper measures immediately to prove the existence of the defect, it is presumed that the defect asserted did not exist at the time of the delivery.

If the thing forwarded will easily deteriorate, the buyer may sell it with the permission of the authorities, the chamber of commerce, or the notary of the place where the thing is. If it is to the advantage of the seller, the buyer is bound to make such sale, when necessary.

The buyer who sells the thing in accordance with the provisions of the preceding paragraph, must inform the

Title I   Sale

ARTICLES 357 TO 363

seller without delay. If he delays the notice, he is liable to give compensation for damages arising therefrom.

Article 359.—When there is a defect in the thing sold for which, according to the provisions of the five preceding articles, the seller is responsible on a warranty, the buyer has the option to rescind the contract or to ask for a reduction of the price, but when it appears from the circumstances of the case, that a rescission of the contract would constitute an obvious unfairness of the transaction, the buyer is only entitled to a reduction of the price.

Article 360.—In the absence of a quality of the thing sold, which was guaranteed by the seller, the buyer may demand compensation for non-performance, instead of rescission of the contract or of a reduction of the price. The same rule applies if the seller has intentionally concealed a defect in a thing.

Article 361.—If the buyer contends that there is a defect in the thing sold, the seller may fix a reasonable period and notify the buyer to declare within such period whether he rescinds the contract or not.

If the buyer does not rescind the contract within the period specified in the preceding paragraph, the right of rescission is lost.

Article 362.—Rescission of a contract on account of a defect in the principal thing extends to its accessory.

If the accessory alone is defective, rescission may be made by the buyer only in respect to such accessory.

Article 363.—If one of several things sold is defective, rescission may be made by the buyer in respect

Chapter II   *Particular Kinds of Obligations*

THE CHINESE CIVIL CODE

to such defective thing only. If several things are sold for an aggregate price, the buyer is also entitled to a reduction in the aggregate price proportionate to the defective thing.

In the case provided by the preceding paragraph, either party may rescind the whole contract if he is obviously injured through the separation of the defective thing from the others.

Article 364.—When the thing sold is a thing designated only as to its kind, and the thing delivered is defective, the buyer may, instead of rescission of contract or a reduction of price, immediately request the seller to deliver in exchange another thing free from defects.

The seller is also bound to warrant that the thing delivered in exchange under the preceding paragraph is free from defect.

Article 365.—Where there has been delivery of a thing which is defective, the right of the buyer to rescind the contract, or to claim a reduction of the price is extinguished by prescription, if not exercised within six months from the date of delivery.

The provisions of the preceding paragraph do not apply if the seller has intentionally concealed the defect.

Article 366.—An agreement discharging the seller of liability on account of defects in a right or a thing or limiting such liability, is void if the seller has intentionally concealed the defect.

Article 367.—The buyer is bound to pay to the seller the agreed price and to accept delivery of the object sold.

Title I   *Sale*

ARTICLES 364 TO 374

Article 368.—If the buyer has good reason to fear that a third person may assert rights which may deprive the said buyer of the whole or a part of the rights derived from the sale, he may refuse to pay the whole or a part of the price, unless the seller has furnished proper security.

In the cases mentioned in the preceding paragraph, the seller may request the buyer to lodge the price.

Article 369.—Unless otherwise provided by law, by contract or by custom, the delivery of the object sold and the payment of the price shall take place simultaneously.

Article 370.—If a time for the delivery of the object sold has been fixed, such time is presumed to be the time for the payment of the price.

Article 371.—If the delivery of the object sold and the payment of the price are to take place simultaneously, the price must be paid at the place of delivery.

Article 372.—If the price is fixed according to the weight of the thing sold, the weight of the packing is to be deducted. But if it is otherwise provided for by contract or if there is a special custom, such contract or custom shall be followed.

Article 373.—The profits and risks of the object sold pass to the buyer at the time of delivery, unless otherwise provided for by contract.

Article 374.—If the buyer requests that the object sold be delivered at a place other than the place where delivery ought to be made, the risks pass to the buyer at

Chapter II   *Particular Kinds of Obligations*

THE CHINESE CIVIL CODE

the time when the seller delivers the object to the person or institution entrusted with its transportation.

Article 375.—If the risks have passed to the buyer before delivery of the object sold, and the seller incurs any necessary outlay on the object before delivery and after such risks have passed, the buyer is bound to compensate the seller for such outlay in conformity with the provisions concerning Mandate.

If the outlay incurred under the circumstances described in the preceding paragraph was not necessary, the buyer is bound to make compensation in conformity with the provisions concerning Management of Affairs Without Mandate.

Article 376.—If the buyer has given special instructions as to the manner of forwarding the object sold and the seller deviates from those instructions without urgent reason, the seller is responsible to the buyer for any damage resulting therefrom.

Article 377.—When the object of a sale is a right, by virtue of which the seller may possess a certain thing, the provisions of the four preceding articles apply *mutatis mutandis*.

Article 378.—Unless otherwise provided by law, by contract or by custom, the costs of sale are to be borne according to the following rules:

1. The costs of the contract of sale are to be borne by both parties equally;

2. The costs of transferring the right sold, the costs of transporting the object of the sale to the place of

Title I *Sale*

ARTICLES 375 TO 382

performance, and the costs of delivery are to be borne by the seller;

3. The costs of taking delivery of the thing sold, the costs of registration and the costs of forwarding the thing sold to a place other than the place of performance, are to be borne by the buyer.

Part 3.—Redemption

Article 379.—When in the contract of sale, the seller reserves the right of redemption, he may redeem the object sold on returning the price.

If the price for redemption specified in the preceding paragraph has been specially fixed by an agreement, such agreement shall be followed.

The interest on the original price and the profits obtained by the buyer from the object sold are deemed to be set off against each other.

Article 380.—The redemption period cannot exceed five years. If a longer period is provided for in the contract, it shall be reduced to five years.

Article 381.—The person who redeems must reimburse the costs of the sale incurred by the buyer together with the price of redemption.

Costs of redemption must be borne by the person who redeems.

Article 382.—When the seller exercises the right of redemption, he must reimburse the expenses and other beneficial outlays made by the buyer for the improvement

Chapter II   *Particular Kinds of Obligations*

THE CHINESE CIVIL CODE

of the object, in so far as the value of the object has been presently increased thereby.

Article 383.—The buyer is bound to the person who redeems to deliver the object sold along with its accessories.

If, owing to circumstances for which the buyer is responsible, the object sold cannot be delivered, or has been obviously altered, the buyer is bound to make compensation for any damage arising therefrom.

Part 4.—*Particular Kinds of Sale*

Article 384.—A contract of sale on approval is a contract which is concluded subject to the condition precedent of the approval of the object of the sale by the buyer.

Article 385.—In a sale on approval the seller is bound to permit the buyer to examine the object to be sold.

Article 386.—If the object has been examined without being delivered and the buyer has not declared his acceptance within the agreed period, the buyer is deemed to have refused acceptance. The same rule applies, if in the absence of an agreed period the buyer has not declared his acceptance within a reasonable period fixed by the seller.

Article 387.—If a thing has been delivered to be examined and the buyer does not return the thing or declare his refusal within the agreed period, or, in the

Title I   *Sale*

ARTICLES 383 TO 393

absence of an agreed period, within a reasonable period fixed by the seller, the buyer is deemed to have accepted.

If the buyer has paid the whole price or a portion of it, or does in respect to the object any act which is not necessary for examining it, he is deemed to have accepted it.

Article 388.—In a sale according to sample the seller is deemed to warrant that the object delivered will conform with the sample.

Article 389.—A clause in a contract of sale by instalments that the whole of the price shall become due as soon as the buyer is in default cannot be enforced, unless the buyer is in default for at least two consecutive instalments representing at least one-fifth of the total price.

Article 390.—In a sale by instalments, if it is agreed that, upon the rescission of the contract, the seller may retain the instalments received, the amount retained cannot exceed an amount representing the rent of the object sold plus damages in case the object sold has sustained any injury.

Article 391.—A sale by auction is concluded when the auctioneer announces its completion by knocking down the hammer or in any other customary manner.

Article 392.—The auctioneer cannot bid nor employ any person to bid at any auction conducted by him.

Article 393.—Unless the person who has ordered the sale has expressed a contrary intention, the auctioneer has the right to adjudge the lot to the highest bidder.

| Chapter II | Particular Kinds of Obligations |

THE CHINESE CIVIL CODE

Article 394.—The auctioneer can omit the announcement of the completion of the sale, and withdraw a lot from the auction if he thinks that the highest bid is insufficient.

Article 395.—A bid made by a bidder ceases to be binding, when a higher bid is made or when the lot is withdrawn from the auction.

Article 396.—The buyer at a sale by auction must pay the price in cash on the completion of the sale or at the time fixed by the notice advertising the sale.

Article 397.—If the buyer at a sale by auction fails to pay the price in time, the auctioneer may rescind the contract and resell the thing by auction.

If the nett proceeds of the second auction do not cover the price and costs of the original auction, the original buyer is liable for the difference.

Title II   *Exchange*

ARTICLES 394 TO 399

TITLE II.—EXCHANGE

Article 398.—The provisions concerning Sale apply *mutatis mutandis* to the case where the parties agree to transfer to one another the ownership of property other than money.

Article 399.—If one of the parties has agreed to deliver or transfer to the other money in addition to the ownership of property specified in the preceding article, the provisions concerning the sale price apply *mutatis mutandis* to such money.

Chapter II   *Particular Kinds of Obligations*

THE CHINESE CIVIL CODE

TITLE III.—CURRENT ACCOUNT

Article 400.—Current account is a contract whereby the parties agree that the claims and debts arising from transactions between them shall be settled at fixed periods and set off against each other, the balance only being paid.

Article 401.—The entry of a bill of exchange, promissory note, cheque or other negotiable instrument in a current account may be cancelled, if such negotiable instrument is not paid by its debtor.

Article 402.—In the absence of a special agreement, the period for striking the balance of a current account shall be six months.

Article 403.—Unless otherwise provided for by contract, either party may at any time terminate the contract of current account and have the balance struck.

Article 404.—The parties may agree that each item in the current account shall bear interest from the date of entry.

Interest may be claimed on the difference from the day the balance was struck.

Article 405.—Cancellation or correction of an entry in a current account cannot be claimed after one year has elapsed from the date when the balance was struck.

Title IV   *Gift*

ARTICLES 400 TO 411

TITLE IV.—GIFT

Article 406.—A gift becomes effective when one of the parties expresses his intention to deliver his property gratuitously to another party and the latter agrees to accept it.

Article 407.—The gift of a property, the transfer of which is subject to registration, is not valid until it has been registered.

Article 408.—So long as the object of the gift has not been delivered to the donee, the donor may revoke the gift. If the thing given has been partially delivered, the donor may revoke the gift for the undelivered portion.

The provision of the preceding paragraph does not apply to gifts executed in writing or to gifts made for the discharge of a moral obligation.

Article 409.—If a gift coming under the provisions of the second paragraph of the preceding article is not executed, the donee may claim the delivery of the thing given or its value, but he is not entitled to interest or other additional damages for such non-execution.

Article 410.—The donor is responsible to the donee only for his intentional acts or gross negligence.

Article 411.—The donor is not liable for a defect in the thing or right given. But, if he has intentionally concealed the defect or expressly warranted that the thing was free from such defect, he is bound to compensate the donee for any damage arising therefrom.

Chapter II   *Particular Kinds of Obligations*

The Chinese Civil Code

Article 412.—If the gift has been made subject to a charge and the donee does not perform the charge after the gift has been delivered to him, the donor may demand compulsory performance or revoke the gift.

If the object of the charge is for public welfare, the competent authorities may, after the death of the donor, order the donee to perform it.

Article 413.—If the gift be subject to a charge and it is not sufficient to defray the charge, the donee is bound to perform the charge only up to the value of the gift.

Article 414.—When a gift is made subject to a charge, the donor is liable for defects in the thing or right given in the same way as a seller, up to the extent of the charge executed by the donee.

Article 415.—If the object of a gift consists in periodical prestations to be performed by the donor, the obligation is extinguished on the death of either the donor or donee, unless the donor has expressed a contrary intention.

Article 416.—The donor may revoke a gift if the donee has acted towards the donor in any of the following ways:—

1. Committing against the donor or his nearest relatives an intentional offence expressly punishable under the Penal Code, or

2. Failing to perform his duty to furnish maintenance to the donor, in case he has such duty.

The right of revocation specified in the preceding

Title IV

Gift

ARTICLES 412 TO 420

paragraph is extinguished by prescription if not exercised within one year from the time when the donor knew of the grounds for revocation. The same rule applies if the donor has expressly forgiven the donee.

Article 417.—The heirs of the donor may revoke the gift if the donee has intentionally and wrongfully caused the death of the donor or prevented the donor from revoking the gift. But their right of revocation will be extinguished by prescription, if not exercised within six months from the time when they knew of the said ground for revocation.

Article 418.—A donor may refuse performance of a gift, if after the gift has been agreed upon his economic conditions have changed to such an extent that the performance of the gift would seriously affect his means of livelihood or hinder his duty to furnish maintenance to others.

Article 419.—Revocation of a gift is made by a declaration of intention to the donee.

After the revocation of the gift, the donor may demand the restitution of the object of the gift in accordance with the provisions concerning Undue Enrichment.

Article 420.—The right of revocation of a gift is extinguished by the death of the donee.

Chapter II   *Particular Kinds of Obligations*

THE CHINESE CIVIL CODE

TITLE V.—LEASE

Article 421.—A lease is a contract whereby the parties agree that one of them shall let the other party use a thing or collect fruits therefrom and the latter shall pay a rent for it.

The rent mentioned in the preceding paragraph may consist of money or of fruits of the thing leased.

Article 422.—A lease of an immovable for a period exceeding one year must be executed in writing. If it is not so executed in writing, it is deemed to have been made for an indefinite period.

Article 423.—The lessor is bound to deliver to the lessee the thing leased in a condition fit for the stipulated use or for the collection of fruits as agreed upon. He is also liable to keep it up in such a condition as to be fit for such use or collection of fruits during the continuance of the lease.

Article 424.—In the case of a lease of a dwelling place or other place intended for habitation, if the defect be such as to endanger the health or security of the lessee or of the persons living with him, the lessee may terminate the contract, although he knew of the defects at the time of the contract or has waived his right of terminating the contract.

Article 425.—The lease continues to exist against the transferee even if the lessor transfer the ownership of the thing leased to a third person after the delivery of the thing.

Title V   *Lease*

ARTICLES 421 TO 431

Article 426.—The provisions of the preceding article shall apply *mutatis mutandis,* when the lessor encumbers the thing leased with a real right, which hinders the thing leased from being used by the lessee.

Article 427.—All charges and taxes on the thing leased are to be borne by the lessor.

Article 428.—If the thing leased is an animal, the lessee shall bear the cost of provender.

Article 429.—Unless otherwise provided for by contract or by custom, the lessor shall make all repairs to the thing leased.

The lessee is bound to allow the lessor to do such acts as are necessary for the maintenance of the thing leased.

Article 430.—If, during the continuance of the lease, the thing leased is in need of repairs incumbent on the lessor, the lessee may fix a reasonable period and notify the lessor to make such repairs. If the lessor fails to make such repairs within that period, the lessee may terminate the contract or make the repairs himself. In the latter case, he may either claim from the lessor reimbursement for any expenses incurrred therefor or deduct the said expenses from the rent.

Article 431.—If the lessee incurs any beneficial expenses for the thing leased, whereby its value is increased, and if the lessor knows of the circumstances but fails to express a contrary intention, he is bound to refund to the lessee, upon the termination of the contract,

| Chapter II | Particular Kinds of Obligations |

THE CHINESE CIVIL CODE

expenses in so far as the value of the thing has been presently increased thereby.

The lessee may remove all the attachments affixed to the thing leased, provided that he restores the thing to its former condition.

Article 432.—The lessee is bound to keep and preserve the thing leased with the care of a good administrator. If the thing leased possesses productivity, he is also bound to maintain such productivity.

If the lessee acts contrary to the provision of the preceding paragraph, whereby loss or damage has been caused to the thing leased, he is bound to make compensation therefor. However, he is not responsible for any damage or change caused to the thing leased through the use of the thing, or through the collection of fruits therefrom, in the ways as agreed upon or in the ways as are in accordance with the nature of the thing.

Article 433.—The lessee is bound to make compensation for loss or damage to the thing leased, which has been brought about by circumstances for which the persons living with him or any third person, whom he permits to use the thing leased or to collect fruits therefrom, are responsible.

Article 434.—If, owing to gross negligence of the lessee, loss or damage is caused by fire to the thing leased, the lessee is bound to compensate the lessor for such loss or damage.

Article 435.—If, in consequence of circumstances for which the lessee is not responsible, the thing leased is

Title V   *Lease*

ARTICLES 432 TO 438

partially destroyed during the continuance of the lease, the lessee may ask for a reduction of rent proportionate to the part destroyed.

In the case specified in the preceding paragraph, if the lessee cannot with the remaining part accomplish the purpose of the lease, he is entitled to terminate it.

Article 436.—If, through the claim of rights by a third person, the agreed use of, or collection of fruits from the thing leased becomes impossible, the provisions of the preceding article apply *mutatis mutandis*.

Article 437.—During the continuance of the lease, if the thing leased is in need of repairs incumbent upon the lessor, or if a preventive measure becomes necessary for avoiding a danger to the thing, or if a third person claims a right over it, the lessee must immediately notify the lessor of the occurrence, unless the lessor already knew of it.

If the lessee delays giving such notice, and where the lessor owing to the delay could not afford remedy in time, the lessee is bound to compensate the lessor for any damage arising therefrom.

Article 438.—The lessee may use the thing leased or collect fruits therefrom only in the ways as are agreed upon, or, in the absence of such agreement, only in the ways as are in accordance with the nature of the thing leased.

If the lessee uses the thing leased or collects fruits therefrom in a way contrary to the provisions of the preceding paragraph, and if he continues to so use it

Chapter II   *Particular Kinds of Obligations*

THE CHINESE CIVIL CODE

notwithstanding a remonstrance of the lessor, the latter may terminate the contract.

Article 439.—The lessee must pay the rent at the agreed time and in the absence of such agreed time, according to custom; and in the absence of such agreement or custom, the rent must be paid at the termination of the lease. If the rent is fixed by periods of time, it must be paid upon the expiration of each of the periods. If there is a season for the collection of fruits from the thing leased, rent must be paid at the end of such season.

Article 440.—If the lessee is in default in respect of payment of rent, the lessor may fix a reasonable period and notify him to pay. If the lessee does not pay within such period, the lessor may terminate the lease.

If the thing leased is a house, the lease cannot be terminated so long as the total rent in arrears does not correspond to two terms.

Article 441.—The lessee is not released from his obligation to pay his rent by the fact that he is prevented from using the thing leased or from collecting fruits therefrom, either wholly or partially, through a cause brought about by himself.

Article 442.—In case the thing leased is an immovable, either party may apply to the Court for an increase or reduction of its rent in proportion to the fluctuation of its value, unless the lease is made for a definite period of time.

Article 443.—The lessee is not entitled to sublet the thing leased to another person without the consent of the

Title V *Lease*

ARTICLES 439 TO 446

lessor. But if the thing leased is a house, the lessee may sublet a part of it to another person, unless otherwise agreed upon.

If the lessee sublets the thing leased to another person contrary to the provisions of the preceding paragraph, the lessor may terminate the lease.

Article 444.—If the lessee sublets the thing leased to another person in conformity with the provisions of the preceding article, the lease is still continuous between the lessor and the lessee.

The lessee is bound to make compensation for damages arising from circumstances for which the sub-lessee is responsible.

Article 445.—The lessor of an immovable has for his claims arising from the lease a right of retention over the movables belonging to the lessee and fixed to the immovable, except those movables which cannot be seized in execution.

In the case of the preceding paragraph, the lessor may compensate himself out of the thing retained only to the extent of those damages he is already entitled to claim for, together with the rent for the present term and for the unpaid past terms.

Article 446.—The lessor's right of retention as specified in the preceding article, is extinguished by the removal of the things to which it applies, unless the removal has taken place without his knowledge or in spite of his objection.

If the removal takes place in the execution of the

Chapter II   *Particular Kinds of Obligations*

The Chinese Civil Code

business or in the ordinary course of life of the lessee, or if the things remaining on the premises are sufficient to guarantee the payment of the rent, the lessor cannot object to the removal.

Article 447.—The lessor may, even without application to the Court, prevent the removal of the things subject to his right of retention, in so far as he is entitled to object to the removal. If the lessee runs away, the lessor is entitled to take possession of the things subject to the right of retention.

If the said things have been removed without the knowledge of or in spite of the objection of the lessor, the lessor may terminate the lease.

Article 448.—The lessee is entitled to uplift the right of retention exercised by the lessor by giving security. He is also entitled to extinguish the right of retention against any individual thing by giving security to the extent of the value of the thing.

Article 449.—The period of a lease cannot exceed twenty years. If it is made for a longer period, such period is to be reduced to twenty years.

The period specified in the preceding paragraph may be renewed by the parties.

Article 450.—When the lease is made for a definite period, the lease terminates at the expiration of such period.

If no time has been specified for the termination of the lease, each party may terminate it at any time. However, if the custom is in favour of the lessee, such custom shall be followed.

Title V *Lease*

ARTICLES 447 TO 455

To terminate a lease as specified in the preceding paragraph a notice must be given in advance according to custom, but if the rent of an immovable is payable weekly, fortnightly or monthly, termination is effective only at the end of the calendar week, or fortnight, or month, and notice must be given at least one week or fortnight or month in advance.

Article 451.—If, after the expiration of the lease, the lessee still continues to use the thing leased or to collect fruits therefrom, and the lessor does not immediately declare his intention to the contrary, the lease is deemed to be continued for an indefinite period.

Article 452.—If the lessee dies, his heirs may terminate the lease by giving notice in accordance with the provisions of paragraph 3 of Article 450, even if the lease was for a definite period of time.

Article 453.—If the lease is made for a definite period and if it is agreed that one of the parties may terminate the lease before its expiration, notice of such termination must be given in advance according to the provisions of paragraph 3 of Article 450.

Article 454.—If the lease is terminated in accordance with the provisions of the two preceding articles, the lessor must return the rent which he has received in advance for those terms falling due after such termination.

Article 455.—The lessee is bound, at the expiration of the lease, to return the thing leased. If the thing leased possesses productivity, he is also bound to return the thing in a state of normal productivity.

Chapter II   *Particular Kinds of Obligations*

THE CHINESE CIVIL CODE

Article 456.—Claims by the lessor against the lessee for compensation for damages caused to the thing leased, and claims by the lessee for the reimbursement of expenses, and his right for the removal of the work done to the thing leased, are extinguished by prescription if not exercised within two years.

The period as specified in the preceding paragraph runs for the lessor from the time when he accepts the return of the thing leased, and for the lessee from the time of the expiration of the lease.

Article 457.—The lessee of an agricultural land is entitled to a reduction or exemption of the rent, if by reason of *force majeure,* the fruits of the thing leased have decreased or totally failed.

The right to claim a reduction or exemption of the rent as specified in the preceding paragraph cannot be waived beforehand.

Article 458.—The lessor of an agricultural land may terminate the lease for the purpose of restoring such land for his own cultivation.

Article 459.—In addition to the provisions of the preceding article and of Article 440, the lessor may terminate the lease only if the lessee acts contrary to the provisions of Article 432, of paragraph 1 of Article 443 or of paragraph 2 of Article 462.

Article 460.—Termination of the lease made by the lessor of an agricultural land takes effect only after the season when the crops are reaped, and before the beginning of the next cultivation.

Title V   *Lease*

ARTICLES 456 TO 463

Article 461.—If the lessee of an agricultural land has incurred expenses in view of the production of crops which are to be reaped after the termination of the lease, he is entitled to claim the reimbursement of such expenses from the lessor, provided that his claim does not exceed the value of such crops.

Article 462.—When agricultural implements, livestock, and other accessories are leased together with an agricultural land, an inventory of the same, showing their individual value at the time of the conclusion of the lease, must be made in duplicate, and signed by the parties. Each party must keep a copy of it.

If any of the accessories mentioned in the inventory be lost through a circumstance for which the lessee is responsible, the lessee is bound to supply substitutes for same.

Should it be lost through a circumstance for which the lessee is not responsible, substitutes must be provided for by the lessor.

Article 463.—The lessee of an agricultural land who has received accessory articles according to an inventory must return them to the lessor at the expiration of the lease. If he fails to do so, he is bound to compensate for their value, as fixed in the aforesaid inventory, less a reduction corresponding to ordinary wear and tear, resulting from their use.

Chapter II   *Particular Kinds of Obligations*

The Chinese Civil Code

Title VI.—Loan

Part 1.—Loan for Use

Article 464.—A contract of loan for use is a contract whereby the parties agree that one of them shall let the other party have gratuitously the use of a thing and the latter shall return it after using it.

Article 465.—A contract of loan for use takes effect only on delivery of the thing lent.

Article 466.—If the lender intentionally conceals a defect in the thing lent, he is responsible to the borrower for any injury resulting therefrom.

Article 467.—The borrower may use the thing lent only in the ways as are agreed upon, or, in the absence of such agreement, only in the ways as are in accordance with the nature of the thing lent.

He is not entitled to allow a third party to use the thing lent without the consent of the lender.

Article 468.—The borrower is bound to preserve the thing lent with the care of a good administrator.

If the borrower acts contrary to the provision of the preceding paragraph whereby loss or damage has been caused to the thing lent, he is bound to make compensation therefor. However, he is not responsible for any change or injury brought about through use of the thing lent in the ways as are agreed upon or as are in accordance with the nature of the thing.

Article 469.—The borrower must bear the ordinary

Title VI   Loan

ARTICLES 464 TO 472

expenses for the maintenance of the thing borrowed. The same rule applies to the cost of provender in the case of a loan of animals.

The borrower may remove any additions to the thing lent which he has made, provided that he restores the thing lent to its former condition.

Article 470.—The borrower is bound to return the thing lent at the expiration of the agreed time. If no time is agreed upon, the thing shall be returned after the borrower has made use of it for the purposes of the loan. The lender may also demand the return of the thing when a reasonable time has elapsed and it may be presumed that the borrower did make use of it.

If the duration of the loan is not fixed and cannot be inferred from the purposes of the loan, the lender may claim the return of the thing at any time.

Article 471.—When several persons have borrowed a thing together, they are jointly responsible to the lender.

Article 472.—The borrower may terminate the loan in any of the following circumstances:—

1. If he has need of the thing lent in consequence of an unforeseen circumstance.

2. If the borrower uses the thing lent otherwise than for the agreed use or for the ordinary uses in accordance with the nature of the thing, or allows a third party to use it without the consent of the lender.

3. If the borrower causes injury or danger of injury to the thing lent by neglecting to take care of it.

4. If the borrower dies.

Chapter II   *Particular Kinds of Obligations*

THE CHINESE CIVIL CODE

Article 473.—A claim for damages by the lender for injury caused to the thing lent, a claim for damages by the borrower in accordance with the provisions of Article 466, and the borrower's right to remove any addition from the thing lent, are extinguished by prescription if not exercised within six months.

The period specified under the preceding paragraph runs for the lender from the time when he accepts the return of the thing lent and for the borrower from the time of the termination of the contract.

Part 2.—Loan for Consumption

Article 474.—A contract of loan for consumption is a contract whereby the parties agree that one of them shall transfer to the other party the ownership of money or other fungible things, and the latter shall return things of the same kind, quality and quantity.

Article 475.—A contract of loan for consumption is effective only on delivery of the money or other fungible things lent.

Article 476.—When interest or other remuneration has been agreed upon for a loan for consumption and when the thing lent is defective, the lender must exchange it for another free from defect. However, the borrower can still claim damages.

When the loan is gratuitous and when the thing lent is defective, the borrower may return to the lender the value which the defective thing had.

In the case of the preceding paragraph, the borrower

Title VI   *Loan*

Articles 473 to 480

can still claim damages when the lender has intentionally concealed the defect.

Article 477.—Interest or remuneration must be paid at the agreed time. In the absence of such agreement, interest or remuneration is payable at the termination of the loan; but, if the loan is to continue for over one year, it is payable at the end of each year.

Article 478.—The borrower shall return things of the same kind, quality and quantity as borrowed, within the agreed time. If no time for such return has been agreed upon, the borrower may return the things at any time, and the lender may fix a reasonable period of not less than one month, and notify the borrower to return the things within such period.

Article 479.—If the borrower cannot return things of the same kind, quality and quantity as borrowed, he must reimburse their value at the time and place where the return ought to have taken place.

If no time or place of return has been agreed upon, such things must be reimbursed according to the value of the things at the time when, or place where they were when the contract was concluded.

Article 480.—Unless otherwise provided for by contract, the following rules shall apply for the repayment of money loans:—

1. When the loan has been made in a currency which is no longer in vogue at the time of repayment, it must be reimbursed in a currency which is in vogue at the time of repayment.

Chapter II *Particular Kinds of Obligations*

THE CHINESE CIVIL CODE

2. A loan which is agreed to be calculated in a currency in vogue must be reimbursed at any cost in a currency in vogue at the time of repayment, irrespective of the fluctuation in the value of the currency which the borrower may have accepted.

3. If a loan is agreed to be calculated in a particular kind of currency, it must be reimbursed in the same kind of currency or in a currency in vogue according to the market rate at the time and place of repayment.

Article 481.—Notwithstanding any agreement to the contrary, if a loan of money is made in goods or other things, the loan is considered to be for a sum equal to the market value of the goods or things at the time and place of delivery.

Title VII   *Hire of Services*

ARTICLES 481 TO 486

TITLE VII.—HIRE OF SERVICES

Article 482.—A contract of hire of services is a contract whereby the parties agree that one of them shall render services for a fixed or undefined period of time to the other party, and the latter shall pay a remuneration.

Article 483.—Remuneration is deemed to have been agreed upon, if according to the circumstances the prestation of services is not to take place without remuneration.

If the amount of the remuneration is not agreed upon, the remuneration shall be paid according to the tariff. If there is no tariff, the remuneration shall be paid according to custom.

Article 484.—The employer cannot transfer his right to the services to a third person without the consent of the employee, and the employee may not have a third person render the services in his place without the consent of the employer.

If either party acts contrary to the provision of the preceding paragraph, the other party may terminate the contract.

Article 485.—If the employee either expressly or impliedly warrants special skill on his part, the absence of such skill entitles the employer to terminate the contract.

Article 486.—The remuneration is payable at the agreed time, and, in the absence of an agreement, according to custom. In the absence of an agreement or custom, the following rules shall apply:—

Chapter II   *Particular Kinds of Obligations*

THE CHINESE CIVIL CODE

1. If the remuneration is fixed by periods, it is payable at the expiration of each period.

2. If the remuneration is not fixed by periods, it is payable at the end of the service.

Article 487.—If the employer is in default in respect to the acceptance of the services, the employee is entitled to his remuneration without being bound to perform the service subsequently. The employer is, however, entitled to deduct from the amount of the remuneration the expenses that the employee has saved by non-performance, and what the employee has gained, or could have gained but for his intentional omission, by rendering services to other persons.

Article 488.—If the duration of services is fixed, the contract terminates with the expiration of that duration.

If the duration of the services is not fixed and cannot be inferred from the nature or object of the services, either party may terminate the contract at any time. However, if there is a custom in favour of the employee, such custom shall be followed.

Article 489.—Even though the duration of the hire of services has been agreed upon, either party can, in the event of any serious occurrence, terminate the contract before the expiration of such duration.

If the occurrence as specified in the preceding paragraph be due to the fault of one of the parties, the other party is entitled to claim damages from him.

Title VIII   *Hire of Work*

ARTICLES 487 TO 493

TITLE VIII.—HIRE OF WORK

Article 490.—A contract of hire of work is a contract whereby one of the parties agrees to execute a definite work for the other party, who agrees to pay him a remuneration after the completion of the work.

Article 491.—Remuneration is deemed to have been agreed upon, if according to the circumstances the execution of the work is not to take place without remuneration.

If the amount of the remuneration is not agreed upon, the remuneration shall be paid according to the tariff. If there is no tariff, the remuneration shall be paid according to custom.

Article 492.—The contractor is bound to execute the work in such a manner that the result has the agreed qualities and is not affected with defects which destroy or reduce its value or its fitness for ordinary purposes or for the purposes mentioned in the contract.

Article 493.—If there be any defect in the work, the employer may fix a reasonable time and notify the contractor to rectify the defect within such time.

If the contractor fails to rectify the defect within the time specified in the preceding paragraph, the employer himself may rectify the defect and claim from the contractor the reimbursement of the necessary expenses arising therefrom.

If the rectification of the defect would require a disproportionate outlay, the contractor may refuse to rectify the defect, and the provisions of the preceding paragraph shall not apply.

Chapter II   *Particular Kinds of Obligations*

The Chinese Civil Code

Article 494.—When the contractor fails to rectify the defect within the time specified in the first paragraph of the preceding article, or refuses to rectify the defect according to the provisions of paragraph 3 of the preceding article, or when the rectification of the defect is impossible, the employer may rescind the contract or demand a reduction of the remuneration. If, however, the defect is of comparatively little importance, or when the contract is for the erection of a structure or other works executed on land, the employer is not entitled to a rescission of the contract.

Article 495.—When the defect is due to circumstances for which the contractor is responsible, the employer may demand damages in addition to the rectification of the defect, or the rescission of the contract, or the reduction of the price as specified in the two preceding articles.

Article 496.—If the defect of the work is due to the nature of the materials supplied by the employer, or to the employer's instructions, the employer forfeits his rights under the three preceding articles, unless the contractor knew of the nature of the materials or of the faulty instructions and failed to notify same to the employer.

Article 497.—If through his own fault, the contractor proceeds with the work in such a manner that it clearly appears that the work will be defective or contrary to the terms of the contract, the employer may fix a reasonable time and notify the contractor to improve the work or to comply with the terms of the contract within such time.

Title VIII　　　　　　　　　　　Hire of Work

ARTICLES 494 TO 562

If the contractor fails to comply with the notice within the time specified, the employer may rectify the defect or have the work continued by a third party at the risks and expenses of the contractor.

Article 498.—The rights of the employer as specified in Articles 493 to 495 can be asserted only if the defects have been discovered within one year after the delivery of the work.

If by reason of the nature of the work, no delivery can take place, the one year period aforementioned runs from the completion of the work.

Article 499.—In case of structures or other works executed on land, and of important repairs to the said structures or works, the period specified in the preceding article shall be extended to five years.

Article 500.—The periods specified in Articles 498 and 499 are extended to five years and ten years respectively in case of defects which the contractor has intentionally concealed.

Article 501.—The periods specified in Articles 498 and 499 may be extended by agreement between the parties, but they cannot be reduced.

Article 502.—If, owing to circumstances for which the contractor is responsible, the work cannot be completed within the agreed time, or, in the absence of such agreement, within a reasonable time, the employer is entitled to a reduction in the remuneration.

In the case specified in the preceding paragraph, if completion or delivery of the work at a fixed time is an

Chapter II *Particular Kinds of Obligations*

THE CHINESE CIVIL CODE

essential element of the contract, the employer may rescind the contract.

Article 503.—If, owing to circumstances for which the contractor is responsible, the work is delayed in such a manner that it can be foreseen that it cannot be completed in time, the employer may rescind the contract, provided that the delay be such as would have entitled him to rescind the contract after the work is completed.

Article 504.—The contractor is not liable for the consequences of delay, if the employer has accepted the work after the delay without reservation.

Article 505.—The remuneration is payable at the time of delivery of the work, or, if no delivery can take place, at its completion.

If the work is to be delivered in parts and a separate remuneration has been specified for each separate part, the remuneration for each part is payable at the time of its delivery.

Article 506.—If, at the time of the making of the contract, only an approximate estimate has been made for remuneration, and if, owing to circumstances for which the employer is not responsible, the remuneration will greatly exceed the estimate, the employer may rescind the contract either during the execution of the work or after its completion.

In the case specified in the preceding paragraph if the contract is for the erection of a structure or other works executed on land, or for important repairs of the said structure or works, the employer is only entitled to a

| *Title VIII* | *Hire of Work* |

ARTICLES 503 TO 509

reasonable reduction of the remuneration; or, if the work is not completed, he may notify the contractor to cease work and may rescind the contract.

When the employer rescinds the contract in accordance with the provisions of the two preceding paragraphs, he is bound to pay to the contractor a reasonable compensation.

Article 507.—If an act of the employer is necessary for the execution of the work and the employer fails to do it, the contractor may fix a reasonable time and notify the employer to do the act within such time.

If the employer fails to do the act within the time specified in the preceding paragraph, the contractor may rescind the contract.

Article 508.—The contractor bears the risk of loss or deterioration of the work before its acceptance by the employer. If the employer is in default of acceptance, the risk passes on to him.

The contractor is not responsible for loss or deterioration by *force majeure* of materials supplied by the employer.

Article 509.—If, before its acceptance by the employer, the work is lost or damaged, or cannot be completed on account of defects in the materials supplied by him or on account of his wrong instructions, and if the contractor has, in time, notified the employer of such defects or such wrong instructions, the contractor is entitled to receive a part of the remuneration proportionate to the labour performed, and reimbursement of any

Chapter II   *Particular Kinds of Obligations*

The Chinese Civil Code

outlay incurred. The contractor is also entitled to damages for further injury if the employer is at fault.

Article 510.—In the case of acceptance provided for in the two preceding articles, if the nature of the work is such that delivery is impossible, the time of completion of the work takes the place of the time of acceptance.

Article 511.—The employer may terminate the contract at any time before the completion of the work by paying damages to the contractor for any injury resulting from such termination.

Article 512.—If the personal skill of the contractor constitutes an essential element of the contract, the contract terminates when the contractor dies or when without fault of his own he becomes incapable of carrying out the work agreed upon.

If a part of the work already done is useful to the employer, he is bound to accept it and to pay a reasonable remuneration for it.

Article 513.—When the contract of hire of work is for the erection of a structure or other works executed on land or for important repairs executed on such structure or works, the contractor has for his claims arising from the contract a right of mortgage on the immovables of the employer upon which the work is done.

Article 514.—The right of the employer to claim for the rectification of a defect, or for the reimbursement of expenses made for the rectification of defect, or for a reduction of the remuneration, or for a rescission of the

Title VIII   *Hire of Work*

ARTICLES 510 TO 514

contract, is extinguished by prescription if not exercised within one year from the discovery of the defect.

The right of the contractor to claim for damages or to rescind the contract is extinguished by prescription if not exercised within one year from the occurrence of the causes on which such claim is based.

Chapter II 　　　　*Particular Kinds of Obligations*

THE CHINESE CIVIL CODE

TITLE IX.—PUBLICATION

Article 515.—A contract for publication is a contract whereby one of the parties agrees to deliver to the other for publication a literary, scientific or artistic work, and the latter agrees to print and circulate the said work.

Article 516.—The rights of the author are transferred to the editor, in so far as it is necessary for the execution of the contract.

The person ceding the right of publication must warrant that, at the time when the contract is concluded, he has the right of ceding the publication; and, if the work is protected by law, he must also warrant that he has its copyright.

If the whole or a part of the work has already been delivered to a third party for publication, or has been published by such third party to the knowledge of the person ceding the right of publication, such person ought to inform the editor about it before the conclusion of the contract.

Article 517.—So long as the copies which the editor is entitled to print and circulate are not exhausted, the person ceding the right of publication cannot dispose to the prejudice of the editor of the whole work or of any part of it.

Article 518.—If the number of editions has not been fixed, the editor is entitled to print only one edition.

If according to the contract, the editor is entitled to publish several editions or to publish the work indefinitely and he neglects to print a new edition after the last one

134

Title IX *Publication*

ARTICLES 515 TO 521

is exhausted, the Court may, on the application of the person ceding the right of publication, order that a new edition be published by the editor within a fixed period. Failure by the editor to comply with this order within such period deprives him of his right of publication.

Article 519.—The editor cannot add or abbreviate or modify the work.

The editor must produce the work in suitable form. He must also make the necessary advertisements and take the customary measures to ensure the diffusion of the work.

The selling price of the publication is to be fixed by the editor, but it must not be fixed too high so as to hinder the sale of the publication.

Article 520.—The author is entitled to correct or improve his work in so far as it does not harm the interests of the editor, or does not increase his responsibility. However, he is bound to make compensation to the editor for all unexpected expenses resulting therefrom.

The editor must give the author the opportunity to correct or improve the work, before a new edition is printed.

Article 521.—Where several works of one and the same author are delivered to the editor to be published separately, the editor is not entitled to publish them collectively.

Where works are delivered by the author to the editor to be published collectively, the editor is not entitled to publish them separately.

Chapter II   *Particular Kinds of Obligations*

THE CHINESE CIVIL CODE

Article 522.—Unless otherwise agreed upon, the right of translation of the work still remains with the person ceding the right of publication.

Article 523.—Remuneration is deemed to have been agreed upon, if from the circumstances the delivery of the work is not to take place without remuneration.

If the editor has the right to publish several editions, the terms relating to remuneration and other conditions for publishing the subsequent editions are presumed to be the same as those of the previous one.

Article 524.—Remuneration is payable when the printing of the whole work is completed, if it is to be issued as a whole, or when the printing of each part is completed if it is to be issued separately.

When the whole or a part of the remuneration is to be fixed according to the results of the sale, the editor is bound to pay such remuneration on setting out his account of sale and to produce proof of same, in conformity with custom.

Article 525.—When the work, after having been delivered to the editor, is lost by *force majeure,* the editor is still liable for the payment of the remuneration.

If the author keeps a duplicate copy of the work lost, he is bound to deliver it to the editor; but in case there is no duplicate, he is bound to remake it, if the work does not entail much labour.

In the case specified in the preceding paragraph, the author may claim a reasonable compensation.

Article 526.—If, previous to the putting into circulation, the whole or a part of the edition is lost by

Title X *Mandate*

ARTICLES 528 TO 538

Article 534.—The mandatory who has a general mandate may on behalf of his principal do all juristic acts, except the following for which a special authority is required:—

1. To sell immovable property or create a real right over it;
2. To lease immovable property for a period of more than two years;
3. To make a gift;
4. To make a compromise;
5. To enter an action in Court;
6. To submit a dispute to arbitration.

Article 535.—The mandatory is bound to manage the affairs entrusted to him in accordance with the instructions of the principal and to do so with such care as he would exercise over his own affairs. If the mandate be non-gratuitous, the affairs must be managed with the care of a good administrator.

Article 536.—A mandatory is not entitled to deviate from the instructions of his principal except in cases of urgency, and provided that from the circumstances he can assume that the principal would approve of the deviation, if he had knowledge of the state of affairs.

Article 537.—The mandatory must attend personally to the affairs entrusted to him. However, if the principal, or a custom, or unavoidable circumstances allow him to do so, he may commission a third person to attend to the said affairs.

Article 538.—If the mandatory has commissioned a

Chapter II

Particular Kinds of Obligations

The Chinese Civil Code

third person to attend to the affairs which are the object of the mandate contrary to the provisions of the preceding article, he is liable for the acts of such third person in the same way as for his own.

If the third person has been commissioned to attend to the affairs in accordance with the provisions of the preceding article the mandatory is liable only for the selection of such third person, and the instructions which he has given to the third person.

Article 539.—When a third person has been commissioned to attend to the affairs which are the object of the mandate, the principal has a direct claim against such third person in respect to the execution of the mandate.

Article 540.—The mandatory must keep the principal informed of the progress of the affairs entrusted to him. He must render a true and detailed account at the expiration of the mandate.

Article 541.—The mandatory must hand over to the principal the moneys, things and fruits which he receives or collects in connection with the management of the affairs of the principal.

He must transfer to the principal the rights which he acquires in his own name but on behalf of the principal.

Article 542.—If the mandatory has used for his own benefit money which he ought to have handed over to his principal or to have used in the interest of the principal, he must pay interest thereon from the day when he used it for his own benefit. He is also bound to make compensation for damages, if any.

Title X   *Mandate*

ARTICLES 539 TO 547

Article 543.—The principal cannot transfer to a third party the claim for management of the affairs without the consent of the mandatory.

Article 544.—The mandatory is liable to the principal for any injury resulting from his negligence in the execution of the mandate or from such acts as are in excess of his authority.

However, if the mandate is gratuitous, the mandatory is liable only for his gross negligence.

Article 545.—The principal must, if required by the mandatory, advance him such sums as are necessary for the execution of the mandate.

Article 546.—If the mandatory, in the execution of the mandate, has incurred necessary expenses, the principal is bound to reimburse them with interest from the day when they were made.

If the mandatory in the execution of the mandate has assumed a necessary obligation, he may require the principal to perform such obligation in his place; or if the obligation is not yet matured, he may require the principal to give proper security for its performance.

If, in the execution of the mandate, the mandatory has suffered injury through a circumstance for which he is not responsible, he is entitled to claim damages from the principal.

Article 547.—Although remuneration has not been agreed upon, the mandatory is entitled to such remuneration as is customary or as may be implied from the nature of the affairs entrusted to him.

Chapter II   *Particular Kinds of Obligations*

THE CHINESE CIVIL CODE

Article 548.—When the mandatory is entitled to a remuneration, it is not payable until the mandate has come to an end and after the mandatory has rendered his accounts, unless otherwise provided for by contract.

If, owing to circumstances for which the mandatory is not responsible, the mandate terminates before the completion of the management of the affairs, the mandatory is entitled to claim remuneration for such part he has managed.

Article 549.—Either party to a contract of mandate can terminate it at any time.

The party who terminates the mandate at a time which is prejudicial to the other party is liable to such party for any injury resulting therefrom, unless the termination has to take place through reasons for which the party terminating the mandate is not responsible.

Article 550.—The mandate terminates when one of the parties dies, or becomes bankrupt, or loses his disposing capacity, unless it is otherwise provided for by contract, or unless, from the nature of the affair, such mandate cannot come to an end.

Article 551.—In the case specified in the preceding article, when it is feared that the extinction of the mandate would be prejudicial to the interest of the principal, the mandatory, his heirs or his statutory agents must continue the management of the affairs, until the principal, his heirs or his statutory agents themselves can take charge of the said affairs.

Article 552.—When the causes for the extinction of

Title X *Mandate*

ARTICLES 548 TO 552

the mandate arise through one of the parties to the contract, the mandate is deemed to continue, until the other party knows or ought to have known of such causes.

Chapter II   *Particular Kinds of Obligations*

The Chinese Civil Code

Title XI.—Manager and Commercial Agents

Article 553.—A manager is a person who has an authority to manage the affairs of a firm and to sign on behalf of the said firm.

The conferring of authority of the manager under the preceding paragraph may be express or implied.

The authority of the manager may be limited to the management of a particular line of business of the firm or to the management of a particular branch or branches of the firm.

Article 554.—As regards third persons a manager is deemed to have authority to do whatever is necessary for the management of the firm, or branch, or line of business entrusted to him.

However, he cannot sell or buy or encumber immovable property, unless he has been given express written authority to do so.

Article 555.—A manager is deemed to have authority to represent his firm in Court as a plaintiff or defendant and to do any other acts of procedure, for the business entrusted to him.

Article 556.—The authority may be given to several managers, but the joint signatures of two of them is binding on the firm.

Article 557.—No limitation to the powers of a manager other than those specified in paragraph 3 of Article 553, paragraph 2 of Article 554, and Article 559, may be set up against third persons acting in good faith.

Title XI   *Manager and Commercial Agents*

ARTICLES 553 TO 561

Article 558.—A commercial agent is a person who, without being a manager, is commissioned by a firm to represent the firm, in the name of the firm, in a particular place or region, either for the whole or for a particular line of business of the firm.

As regards third persons the commercial agent is deemed to have authority to do whatever is necessary for carrying on the business of the firm which he represents.

A commercial agent cannot subscribe negotiable instruments or borrow fungible things or file an action in Court, unless he has been given written authority to do so.

Article 559.—The commercial agent must keep his firm informed of the commercial conditions of his place or district in the line of business entrusted to him. He must report without delay to his firm any transaction which he has made for it.

Article 560.—A commercial agent can claim such remuneration and reimbursement of expenses as agreed upon; or, in the absence of such agreement, he is entitled to such remuneration of expenses as are customary. In the absence of such agreement or custom, his remuneration must be proportionate to the importance and volume of the business which he has transacted for his firm.

Article 561.—If the duration of the authority of the commercial agent is not fixed, either party may terminate it at any time, provided that three months' previous notice is given to the other party.

Each party may also terminate the contract at any time without notice in case the termination has to take place

| Chapter II | Particular Kinds of Obligations |

THE CHINESE CIVIL CODE

through reasons for which the party who terminates the contract is not responsible.

Article 562.—A manager or commercial agent cannot without the consent of his firm enter on his own account or on account of third persons into any business of the same kind as that which he transacts for his firm, nor can he be a partner with unlimited liability in a commercial firm which carries on the same kind of business.

Article 563.—If a manager or commercial agent acts contrary to the provisions specified in the preceding article, his firm is entitled to claim from him, as damages, the profits resulting from the prohibited transaction.

The right to claim under the preceding paragraph is extinguished by prescription if it is not exercised within one month from the time when the firm knew of the contravention or within one year from the date of the act.

Article 564.—The authority of a manager or commercial agent does not terminate, when the principal of the firm dies, becomes bankrupt or loses his disposing capacity.

TITLE XII.—BROKERAGE

Article 565.—A contract of brokerage is a contract whereby one of the parties agrees to inform the other party of the occasion to conclude a contract, or to act as intermediary for the conclusion of a contract, and such other party agrees to pay him a remuneration.

Article 566.—Remuneration is deemed to have been agreed upon, if from the circumstances the broker is not to supply the information for the conclusion of the contract or to act as an intermediary for it without a remuneration.

If the amount of the remuneration is not specified, it shall be paid according to the tariff. If there is no tariff, the remuneration shall be paid according to custom.

Article 567.—The broker is bound to render to each party a true account of the circumstances of the proposed transaction, so far as he knows them. He is not entitled to act as intermediary for a person who is notoriously insolvent or whom he knows to have no capacity to enter into the proposed contract.

Article 568.—The broker is entitled to his remuneration only if the contract is concluded through his intermediary or due to the information supplied by him.

When the contract is concluded under a condition precedent, the broker cannot claim the remuneration until the condition is fulfilled.

Article 569.—The broker is entitled to claim reimbursement for expenses incurred by him only if such reimbursement has been agreed upon.

Chapter II   *Particular Kinds of Obligations*

The Chinese Civil Code

The provisions of the preceding paragraph apply even if no contract is concluded after the broker has supplied the information or acted as an intermediary.

Article 570.—Unless otherwise provided for by contract or by custom, each party to the contract must bear an equal part of the remuneration to which the broker is entitled for having acted as intermediary.

Article 571.—The broker forfeits his rights to a remuneration and to reimbursement of expenses if he acts in the interest of the other party contrary to his obligations to the principal, or if he accepts from such other party advantages under such circumstances as are incompatible with the rules of honesty and good faith.

Article 572.—If the agreed remuneration is out of proportion with the actual value of the services rendered by the broker to such an extent that unfairness of the transaction appears, the Court may at its discretion, on the application of the principal, reduce it to a reasonable amount. But no claim can be made for the return of the remuneration already paid.

Article 573.—An agreement promising a remuneration for matrimonial brokerage is void.

Article 574.—A broker has no authority to make or to receive on behalf of the parties prestations due by virtue of the contract entered into through his intermediary.

Article 575.—The broker is bound, if so instructed by one of the parties, not to disclose the name of such party or of such party's firm to the other party to the contract.

Title XII   *Brokerage*

ARTICLES 570 TO 575

When the broker does not disclose to one of the parties the name of the other party or of the other party's firm, he is personally liable for the performance of the obligations of such other party resulting from the contract and he has authority to receive prestations on behalf of such party.

| Chapter II | Particular Kinds of Obligations |

THE CHINESE CIVIL CODE

TITLE XIII.—COMMISSION AGENCY

Article 576.—A commission agent is a person who undertakes, as a business, to buy or sell movable things or execute any other commercial transaction in his own name but on account of a principal, for a remuneration.

Article 577.—In addition to the provisions contained in the present title, the provisions concerning Mandate apply to Commission Agency.

Article 578.—The commission agent personally acquires rights against and incurs obligations towards the parties with whom he transacts business on account of the principal.

Article 579.—Unless otherwise provided for by contract or by custom, if the other party to a contract, which a commission agent made on behalf of a principal, does not perform his obligations, the commission agent is directly liable to the principal for the execution of the contract.

Article 580.—When a commission agent has made a sale for a lower price or has made a purchase for a higher price than that specified by the principal, and if he takes the burden of reimbursing the difference, the sale or purchase takes effect as against the principal.

Article 581.—If the commission agent concludes a sale for a higher price, or concludes a purchase for a lower price than that specified by the principal, the benefit shall belong to the principal.

Article 582.—The commission agent is entitled to

Title XIII   Commission Agency

ARTICLES 576 TO 585

such remuneration, storage charges and transportation charges as are specified in the contract, or as are customary. He is also entitled to reimbursement with interest of the expenses which he makes in the interest of the principal.

Article 583.—So long as the things bought or sold by the commission agent on account of the principal are in the possession of the commission agent, the rules concerning Deposit apply.

The commission agent is not bound to insure the things mentioned in the preceding paragraph, unless he has been otherwise instructed by the principal.

Article 584.—If goods entrusted to a commission agent for sale arrive in a defective condition, or if owing to their nature they may easily perish, the commission agent is bound to take for the protection of the interests of the principal such steps as he would take for the protection of his own interest.

Article 585.—If the principal refuses to accept the goods bought by the commission agent under orders of the principal, the commission agent may fix a reasonable period and notify the principal to accept within such period. If the principal fails to accept the goods within such period, the commission agent may sell them by auction and appropriate the proceeds of the sale up to the amount due to him by the principal by reason of the contract of commission. The balance, if any, may be lodged.

Goods that will easily perish may be sold without notice.

Chapter II   *Particular Kinds of Obligations*

The Chinese Civil Code

Article 586.—If goods entrusted to a commission agent for sale could not be sold, or if the order to sell has been revoked by the principal, and the principal fails to take back the goods or to dispose of them within a reasonable time, the commission agent may exercise his rights in conformity with the provisions of the preceding article.

Article 587.—Unless there is an agreement to the contrary, the commission agent who has been ordered to buy or sell currency, shares or things which have a market quotation may himself be the seller or buyer, the price being determined in accordance with the market quotation at the time of the sale or purchase made in conformity with the orders of the principal.

The commission agent is entitled to exercise his claims specified in Article 582 even in the case specified in the preceding paragraph.

Article 588.—In cases where the commission agent is entitled to be himself the seller or buyer, if he notifies the principal of the conclusion of the contract without disclosing the name of other party, he is deemed to have assumed personally the obligations of such other party.

Title XIV   *Deposit*

Articles 586 to 593

Title XIV.—Deposit

Article 589.—A contract of deposit is a contract whereby one of the parties delivers a thing to the other party, who agrees to keep it in his custody.

The depositary is not entitled to a remuneration unless otherwise provided for by contract or unless according to the circumstances the keeping into custody is not to be assumed without remuneration.

Article 590.—The depositary is bound to take as much care of the thing deposited as he takes of his own things. If the deposit is undertaken for a remuneration, the depositary is bound to keep the thing in his custody with the care of a good administrator.

Article 591.—The depositary may not use the thing deposited or allow a third party to use it without the consent of the depositor.

The depositary, who acts contrary to the provisions of the preceding paragraph, must pay a reasonable compensation to the depositor. He is also liable for damages, if any, unless he can prove that the damages would have occurred even if the thing had not been used.

Article 592.—The depositary must personally keep the thing deposited. He may, however, entrust its custody to a third party if he is allowed to do so by the depositor, or by custom, or in case of unavoidable necessity.

Article 593.—The depositary who entrusts the custody of the thing deposited to a third party contrary

Chapter II   *Particular Kinds of Obligations*

The Chinese Civil Code

to the provisions of the preceding article is liable for any injury thereby caused to the thing deposited, unless he can prove that the injury would have happened even if the thing deposited had not been entrusted to such third party.

The depositary who entrusts the custody of the thing deposited to a third party in conformity with the provisions of the preceding article is liable only for the selection of such third party and for the instructions which he has given to the said third party.

Article 594.—The depositary may not change the method of custody which has been agreed upon, except in case of urgency when he may assume that the depositor would approve of the change if he knew of the state of affairs.

Article 595.—The depositor is bound to reimburse the depositary for any expenses which were necessary for the preservation or maintenance of the thing deposited. But if it is otherwise agreed upon, such agreement shall apply.

Article 596.—The depositor is liable for any injury caused to the depositary and resulting from the nature or defects of the thing deposited, unless at the time of deposit he did not know of the defect or the dangerous character of the thing and his ignorance was not due to his fault, or unless the depositary knew of them.

Article 597.—Although the parties have fixed a time for the return of the thing deposited, the depositor may still at any time demand the return of it.

Title XIV *Deposit*

Articles 594 to 602

Article 598.—If the parties have fixed no time for the return of the thing deposited, the depositary may return it at any time.

If a time has been fixed, the depositary cannot return the thing deposited before the expiration of that time, except in a case of unavoidable necessity.

Article 599.—The depositary is bound to return together with the thing deposited any fruits which may have accrued from it.

Article 600.—The return of the thing deposited shall be made at the place where the thing was to be kept.

If the depositary has removed the thing to another place in accordance with the provisions of Article 592 or 594, the return may be made at the place where the thing actually is.

Article 601.—If a remuneration has been agreed upon, it is payable at the termination of the deposit. If the remuneration is fixed by periods, it is payable at the end of each period.

If the custody of the thing deposited be suspended owing to a circumstance for which the depositary is not liable, the depositary may claim a portion of the remuneration proportionate to his services rendered, unless otherwise provided for by contract.

Article 602.—In the case of a deposit of fungible things, if it is agreed that the ownership of such things passes to the depositary, and that the depositary shall return things of the same kind, quality and quantity, the provisions concerning Loans for Consumption apply

Chapter II　　　　　　*Particular Kinds of Obligations*

The Chinese Civil Code

from the moment when the things were accepted by the depositary.

Article 603.—If the deposit is one of money, it is presumed that the depositary is not bound to return the original money received, but only the same amount of such money.

If the depositary in conformity with the provision of the preceding paragraph is only bound to return the same amount, the profit and risk of the thing deposited passes to such depositary at the time of its delivery.

In the case provided for in the preceding paragraph, if a period has been fixed for the return of the thing deposited, the depositor cannot claim the return of the thing before the expiration of that period, except in case of unavoidable necessity.

Article 604.—The depositary is bound to return the thing deposited to the depositor, notwithstanding any claim of a third person who asserts a right over it, unless such person files an action against the depositary or attaches the thing.

In the case of an attachment or action by such third person, the depositary must inform the depositor without delay.

Article 605.—Claims for remuneration, reimbursement of expenses or damages relating to a contract of deposit are extinguished by prescription, if not exercised within one year from the date of the termination of the deposit.

Article 606.—The proprietor of a hotel or such other

Title XIV   *Deposit*

ARTICLES 603 TO 610

place where guests are received for lodging is liable for any loss of or injury to the things which a guest has brought with him. The same rules apply even when the loss or injury is caused by third persons.

But he is not liable for loss or injury caused by *force majeure,* or resulting from the nature of the thing, or due to the intentional acts or fault of the guest himself or of his fellow guests or of the servants of the guest or of persons whom the guest has received.

Article 607.—The proprietor of a restaurant or a bath-house, is liable for any loss of or damage to the ordinary things which the guest has brought with him, except in the cases provided for in the second paragraph of the preceding article.

Article 608.—The proprietor is not liable for moneys, valuable securities, jewellery or other valuables, unless they have been deposited with the proprietor with a specification of their nature and quantity.

The proprietor is liable for the loss or injury of the articles specified in the preceding article, which he has refused without justifiable cause to receive into safe custody. The same rule applies when the loss or injury is caused through the intentional acts or fault of the proprietor or of his employees.

Article 609.—A notice, which excludes or limits the liability of the proprietor provided for in the three preceding articles, is void.

Article 610.—The guest must give notice to the proprietor of the loss or injury immediately after knowledge

Chapter II   *Particular Kinds of Obligations*

The Chinese Civil Code

of the same. If he delays giving such notice, he forfeits his right to claim for damages.

Article 611.—The right to claim for damages arising from the provisions of Articles 606 to 608, is extinguished by prescription if not exercised within six months from the date of the discovery of the loss or injury. The same rule applies when six months have elapsed from the departure of the guest.

Article 612.—The proprietor is entitled to retain the luggage or other property of the guest, until he has been paid the whole of what the guest may owe him in respect to lodging, food or other disbursements.

Title XV.—Warehousing

Article 613.—A warehouseman is a person who undertakes, as a business, the storage and custody of goods for other persons, for a remuneration.

Article 614.—In addition to the provisions of the present title, the provisions concerning Deposit apply *mutatis mutandis* to Warehousing.

Article 615.—If required by the depositor, the warehouseman must make out and deliver to him a godown warrant from a warehouse register.

Article 616.—The godown warrant shall contain the following particulars and be signed by the warehouseman:—

1. The name and address of the depositor;
2. The place of storage;
3. The kind of goods stored, their quality and quantity and the kind, number and marking of the packages;
4. The place where and the date when the godown warrant is made out;
5. The period for which the goods are stored, if that has been fixed;
6. The remuneration for storage;
7. If the goods stored are insured, the amount of the insurance, the period for which the goods are insured and the name of the insurer.

The warehouseman must enter the same particulars abovementioned in the counterfoil of the warehouse register.

Chapter II   *Particular Kinds of Obligations*

THE CHINESE CIVIL CODE

Article 617.—The holder of the godown warrant may require the warehouseman to divide the goods stored and to issue to him a separate godown warrant for each part, provided that the holder shall return the original godown warrant to the warehouseman.

The expenses for such division and for the insurance of the new godown warrants specified under the preceding paragraph must be borne by the holder.

Article 618.—The transfer of ownership of the goods entered in a godown warrant is not effective unless the godown warrant has been endorsed by the owner of the goods with the counter-signature of the warehouseman.

Article 619.—The warehouseman cannot request the depositor to remove the goods before the expiration of the time agreed upon for the storage.

If no time has been agreed upon for the storage, the warehouseman may, after six months have elapsed from the commencement of the custody, request at any time, the removal of the goods, provided that one month's previous notice is given to the depositor.

Article 620.—The warehouseman is bound, on the request of the depositor or of the holder of the godown warrant, to allow them to inspect the goods deposited or to take samples.

Article 621.—If, at the termination of the contract of warehousing, the depositor or holder of the godown warrant refuses or is unable to remove the goods deposited, the warehouseman may fix a reasonable time and request the depositor to remove the goods within such time. If

Title XV *Warehousing*

ARTICLES 617 TO 621

the goods are not removed within such time, the warehouseman may sell them by auction, and deduct from the proceeds of the sale the expenses of the auction and the storage charges; the balance, if any, shall be delivered to the person entitled thereto.

Chapter II   *Particular Kinds of Obligations*

The Chinese Civil Code

Title XVI.—Carriage

Part 1.—General Provisions

Article 622.—A carrier is a person who undertakes as a business to transport goods or passengers for freight.

Article 623.—Claims for damages for loss, injury or delay in the transportation of goods or passengers are extinguished by prescription if not exercised within two years from the date of the termination of the transportation, or from the date when the termination of the transportation ought to have taken place.

Part 2.—Carriage of Goods

Article 624.—If required by the carrier, the sender must make and issue to him a way-bill.

The way-bill must contain the following particulars and be signed by the sender:—

1. The name and address of the sender;
2. The kind of the goods sent, their quality and quantity, and the kind, number and marking of the packages;
3. The place of destination;
4. The name and address of the consignee;
5. The place where and the time when the way-bill is made out.

Article 625.—If required by the sender, the carrier must make and issue to him a bill of lading.

Title XVI   *Carriage*

ARTICLES 622 TO 631

The bill of lading must contain the following particulars and be signed by the carrier:—

1.   Those mentioned in sections 1, 2, 3 and 4 of the preceding article.

2.   The amount of freight, and whether it is paid by the sender or is to be paid by the consignee.

3.   The place where and the time when the bill of lading is made out.

Article 626.—The sender must supply the carrier with the documents which are necessary for the transport of the goods or required by the fiscal and police authorities, and furnish the necessary information to that effect.

Article 627.—When a bill of lading has been supplied to the sender, the facts concerning the carriage as between the carrier and the holder of the bill are determined by the tenor of the bill of lading.

Article 628.—Even though a bill of lading has been made out to a named consignee, it can be transferred by indorsement to another person, unless indorsement is forbidden in the bill.

Article 629.—The delivery of the bill of lading to a person entitled to take delivery of the goods has the same effect, as regards the transfer of the ownership of the goods, as the delivery of the goods themselves.

Article 630.—The consignee must, on his requesting the delivery of the goods, surrender the bill of lading.

Article 631.—If the goods are of such a nature as are likely to cause injury to persons or property, the sender

Chapter II   *Particular Kinds of Obligations*

THE CHINESE CIVIL CODE

must declare their nature to the carrier before making the contract of carriage, failing which he shall be liable to make compensation for any injury caused thereby.

Article 632.—The goods must be transported within the agreed time; in the absence of such agreement, custom must rule; and in the absence of such agreement or custom, transportation must be done within a reasonable time.

In determining what is a reasonable time as mentioned in the preceding paragraph, the circumstances of each particular case shall be taken into consideration.

Article 633.—The carrier is not entitled to deviate from the instructions of the sender except in case of urgency, and provided that from the circumstances he can assume that the sender would approve of the deviation if he had knowledge of the state of affairs.

Article 634.—The carrier is liable for any loss, injury or delay in the delivery of the goods entrusted to him, unless he can prove that the loss, injury or delay is due to *force majeure,* or to the nature of the goods, or to the fault of the sender or of the consignee.

Article 635.—The carrier is liable for loss or injury due to apparent defects in packing, if he has accepted the goods for transportation without reservation.

Article 636.—The carrier is liable for loss, injury or delay caused by the fault of his employees or of other persons to whom he entrusted the goods for transportation.

Article 637.—If the goods were transported by several

Title XVI   *Carriage*

ARTICLES 632 TO 641

successive carriers, such of them as are unable to prove that they have no liability under the three preceding articles are jointly liable for the loss, injury or delay.

Article 638.—In the case of loss, injury or delay, the damages shall be fixed in accordance with the value which the goods would have had at the place of destination and at the time when delivery was due.

The freight and other expenses which need not be paid in consequence of the loss of or injury to the goods transported must be deducted from the amount of damages specified in the preceding paragraph.

If the loss, injury or delay is due to the intentional acts or gross negligence of the carrier, the sender may also claim for other injury, if any.

Article 639.—The carrier is not liable for moneys, valuable securities, jewellery or such other valuables, unless he is given notice of the nature and value of such goods when they are entrusted to him.

If their value is declared, the liability of the carrier is limited to such declared value.

Article 640.—Damages in the case of delay in delivery cannot exceed the amount which could be claimed in case of the total loss of the goods.

Article 641.—In the cases of Articles 633, 650 and 651 and in other cases which may prevent or delay the transportation, or imperil the safety of the goods, the carrier must exercise such care and take such measures as are necessary for the protection of the interest of the owner of the goods.

Chapter II   *Particular Kinds of Obligations*

THE CHINESE CIVIL CODE

If he fails to take such care and measures as specified in the preceding paragraph, he is liable for any injury resulting therefrom.

Article 642.—As long as the carrier has not notified the consignee of the arrival of the goods, or the consignee after their arrival has not asked for their delivery, the sender, or, if a bill of lading has been made, the holder of the bill of lading can require the carrier to stop the transportation and to return the goods, or to make any other disposition of them.

In the case provided for in the preceding paragraph, the carrier is entitled to the freight in proportion to the transportation already performed and to all expenses occasioned by the stoppage, return or other disposition of the goods, and to reasonable damages.

Article 643.—The carrier must notify the consignee as soon as the goods arrive.

Article 644.—After the goods have arrived at the place of destination, and the consignee has demanded delivery, the consignee acquires the rights of the sender arising from the contract of carriage.

Article 645.—The carrier is not entitled to the freight of goods which are lost by *force majeure* during transportation. Whatever has been received for that purpose must be returned.

Article 646.—If the carrier delivers the goods before payment of freight and other expenses, he remains liable to the preceding carriers for such part of the freight and other expenses as may still be due to them.

Title XVI   *Carriage*

ARTICLES 642 TO 650

Article 647.—The carrier is entitled to retain such portion of the goods as may be necessary to secure payment of freight and other expenses.

If the amount of the freight and other expenses be disputed, the consignee is entitled to ask for the delivery of the goods on lodging the amount in dispute.

Article 648.—The liability of the carrier ceases when the consignee has, without reservations, accepted the goods and paid the freight and other expenses.

But this does not apply in the case of loss of or injury to the goods not easily discoverable, provided that notice of such loss or injury be given to the carrier within ten days after the goods have been accepted by the consignee.

When the loss or injury has been fraudulently concealed by the carrier, or is due to the carrier's intentional acts or gross negligence, the carrier cannot take advantage of the two preceding paragraphs.

Article 649.—A statement in a receipt, bill of lading or other such document delivered by the carrier to the sender excluding or limiting the liability of the carrier is ineffective, unless it is proved that the sender has expressly agreed to such exclusion or limitation of liability.

Article 650.—If the consignee cannot be found, or if he refuses to take delivery of the goods, the carrier must immediately notify the sender thereof and ask for his instructions.

If the instructions of the sender are impracticable, or if the carrier cannot keep the goods any longer in his custody, the carrier may deposit the goods in a warehouse at the expense of the sender.

Chapter II   *Particular Kinds of Obligations*

THE CHINESE CIVIL CODE

If circumstances are such that deposit in a warehouse is impossible, or if the goods are of a perishable nature, or if it is obvious that their value will not be sufficient to cover the freight and other expenses, the carrier may sell the goods by auction.

So far as is practicable, the carrier must notify the sender and the consignee of the fact of the deposit in the warehouse or of the sale by auction.

Article 651.—The provisions of the preceding article apply, when delay of delivery is due to an action as to who is entitled to take delivery of the goods.

Article 652.—The carrier shall, after deducting from the proceeds of the auction the costs of auction, the freight and other expenses, deliver the surplus to the person entitled to it, or, if such person cannot be found, lodge it for such person's benefit.

Article 653.—If the goods were transported by several successive carriers, the last of them can exercise the rights described in Articles 647, 650 and 652 for the amounts due to them all for freight and other expenses.

Part 3.—Carriage of Passengers

Article 654.—The carrier of passengers is liable for any injury suffered by the passenger in consequence of the transportation, and for delay in the transportation, unless the injury is due to *force majeure* or to the fault of such passenger.

Article 655.—Luggage entrusted to the carrier in time must be delivered on the arrival of the passenger.

Title XVI   *Carriage*

ARTICLES 651 TO 659

Article 656.—If the passenger does not take delivery of the luggage within six months after its arrival, the carrier can sell it by auction.

If the luggage is of a nature that will easily perish, the carrier can sell it by auction forty-eight hours after its arrival.

The provisions of Article 652 apply *mutatis mutandis* to the cases provided for the two preceding paragraphs.

Article 657.—Unless otherwise provided for under this part, the rights and obligations of the carrier for the luggage, which the passenger has entrusted to him, are governed by the provisions concerning Carriage of Goods, even though the carrier did not make a separate charge for it.

Article 658.—The carrier is liable for the loss or injury of the luggage caused by his own fault or that of his employees, even if such luggage has not been entrusted to him by the passenger.

Article 659.—A statement in a ticket, receipt or other document delivered by the carrier to the passenger, excluding or limiting the liability of the carrier, is ineffective, unless it can be proved that the passenger expressly agreed to such exclusion or limitation of liability.

Chapter II　　　　　*Particular Kinds of Obligations*

THE CHINESE CIVIL CODE

TITLE XVII.—FORWARDING AGENCY

Article 660.—A forwarding agent is a person who undertakes, as a business, to forward goods through carriers in his own name but on account of other persons, for a remuneration.

Unless otherwise provided for in this title, the provisions concerning Commission Agents apply *mutatis mutandis* to Forwarding Agency.

Article 661.—The forwarding agent is liable for any loss, injury or delay in the delivery of the goods entrusted to him, unless he can prove that he has not failed to exercise due care in the reception and custody of the goods, in the selection of the carrier, in the delivery at the place of destination and in all other matters connected with the transportation.

Article 662.—The forwarding agent is entitled to retain such portion of the goods, as may be necessary to secure payment of his remuneration and disbursements.

Article 663.—Unless otherwise provided for by contract, the forwarding agent may himself assume the transportation of the goods, in which case he has the same rights and obligations as a carrier.

Article 664.—If a fixed price for the whole of the transportation has been agreed upon, or if the forwarding agent has himself delivered to the sender a bill of lading, the forwarding agent is deemed to have himself assumed the transportation of the goods, in which case he is not entitled to remuneration.

Title XVII   *Forwarding Agency*

ARTICLES 660 TO 666

Article 665.—The provisions of Articles 631, 635, 638, 639 and 640 apply *mutatis mutandis* to Forwarding Agency.

Article 666.—Claims against a forwarding agent for loss, injury or delay in the transportation are extinguished by prescription if not exercised within two years from the date of the delivery of the goods or from the date when such delivery ought to have taken place.

Chapter II *Particular Kinds of Obligations*

The Chinese Civil Code

Title XVIII.—*Partnership*

Article 667.—Partnership is a contract whereby two or more persons agree to put contributions in common for a collective enterprise.

The contribution may consist of money or other things or of services.

Article 668.—The contributions of the members and all other properties of the partnership are held in common by all the members.

Article 669.—Unless there is a special agreement, a partner is not bound to provide an increase of the contribution which has been agreed upon, nor, if his contribution has been reduced by losses, to make good such losses.

Article 670.—Unless otherwise provided for by contract, no change in the original contract of partnership or in the nature of the enterprise may take place, except by the unanimous consent of all the partners.

Article 671.—Unless otherwise provided for by contract, the affairs of the partnership shall be managed by all the partners in common.

When it is agreed upon that the affairs of the partnership shall be managed by some of the members only, the affairs of the partnership shall be managed in common by the said members of the partnership.

The current affairs of the partnership may be managed individually by each partner who has the right of management, but, in such a case, every partner who has the right of management can oppose the action of any other partner.

Title XVIII   *Partnership*

ARTICLES 667 TO 677

In a case of opposition, the execution of the affair must be stopped.

Article 672.—A partner in the fulfilment of the obligations which are incumbent upon him under the partnership contract, must exercise such care as he is accustomed to exercise in his own affairs.

Article 673.—If it is agreed upon that certain matters shall be decided by a majority vote of all the partners in the partnership or of some of them, each partner entitled to vote is presumed to have one vote only, irrespective of the amount of his contribution.

Article 674.—When one or several partners in the partnership have been entrusted with the management of the affairs of the partnership, they cannot resign or be removed by the other partners except for a justifiable cause.

Removal of a managing partner, as specified in the preceding paragraph, can take place only by the unanimous consent of all the other partners.

Article 675.—Notwithstanding any stipulation to the contrary, a partner, who has no right of management is entitled to enquire at any time into the affairs of the partnership and its financial situation, and to examine its books.

Article 676.—Unless otherwise provided for by contract, the accounts of a partnership must be settled and its profits be distributed at the end of each business year.

Article 677.—If the shares of the partners in the

Chapter II | Particular Kinds of Obligations

THE CHINESE CIVIL CODE

profits and losses are not specified, they are fixed in proportion to the contribution of each partner.

If only the share in profits or the share in losses is specified, the proportion is deemed to be applicable to both profits and losses.

Unless otherwise provided for by contract, a member who contributed only his services does not share in the losses.

Article 678.—A partner is entitled to the reimbursement of the expenses which he has made for the affairs of the partnership.

Unless otherwise provided for by contract, he is not entitled to a remuneration for having managed the affairs of the partnership.

Article 679.—A partner who is entrusted with the management of the affairs of the partnership represents the other partners towards third parties, in so far as he manages such affairs in conformity with his original authority.

Article 680.—The provisions of Articles 537 to 546 concerning Mandate apply *mutatis mutandis* to the management of the affairs of the partnership by its partners.

Article 681.—If the assets of the partnership are not sufficient to cover the liabilities, the partners are liable as joint debtors for the deficit.

Article 682.—A partner is not entitled to demand the partition of the assets, until the liquidation of the partnership takes place.

Title XVIII   *Partnership*

ARTICLES 678 TO 687

A debtor of the partnership who has a claim against one of the partners cannot set it off against a claim of the partnership against him.

Article 683.—A partner cannot transfer his share in the partnership to a third person, unless it be to another partner.

Article 684.—So long as the partnership continues, a personal creditor of a partner cannot be subrogated in any of the rights of such partner against the partnership, except claims for dividends.

Article 685.—A creditor of a partner may apply for attachment against the share of such partner, provided that two months' previous notice has been given to the partnership.

The notice under the preceding paragraph, operates as an application for withdrawal of that partner.

Article 686.—If no period has been fixed for the duration of the partnership, or if the partnership has been formed for the lifetime of any of its partners, each partner may withdraw from it, provided that the other partners have been notified two months beforehand.

The withdrawal as specified in the preceding paragraph cannot take place at a time when withdrawal would be prejudicial to the affairs of the partnership.

Even if a period has been fixed for the duration of the partnership, a member may give notice of withdrawal for serious reasons due to circumstances for which he is not responsible.

Article 687.—In addition to the cases provided for in

175

Chapter II   *Particular Kinds of Obligations*

THE CHINESE CIVIL CODE

the two preceding articles, withdrawal of a partner takes place in any of the following:—

1. In the case of his death, unless it has been provided for by contract that his heirs would take his place;

2. In the case of his being declared bankrupt or interdicted;

3. In the case of his exclusion as a partner.

Article 688.—Exclusion of a partner can only take place for a justifiable cause.

The exclusion as specified in the preceding paragraph may be made only by the unanimous consent of the other members, and a notice of the fact must be served on the excluded partner.

Article 689.—The settlement of the accounts between the retiring partner and the other partners must be made on the basis of the financial situation of the partnership at the time of retirement.

The share of the retiring member may be repaid in money, irrespective of the nature of his contribution.

In regard to those affairs of the partnership not yet concluded at the time of retirement, accounts may be settled and profits and losses be distributed after the conclusion of such affairs.

Article 690.—A person who has retired from a partnership continues to be liable in respect of the obligations incurred before his retirement.

Article 691.—No person can be introduced as a partner in a partnership that is already existing, except by the unanimous consent of all the partners.

Title XVIII   *Partnership*

ARTICLES 688 TO 697

A person who becomes a partner of such a partnership is liable in the same way as the other partners for all the obligations incurred prior to his entering it.

Article 692.—A partnership is dissolved in any of the following cases:—

1. When the period agreed upon for its duration has expired;

2. When the partners unanimously decide to dissolve it;

3. When the undertaking which forms its object is accomplished, or when it is impossible to accomplish it.

Article 693.—If, after the expiration of the period agreed upon for the duration of the partnership, the partners continue its affairs, the partnership contract is deemed to continue for an indefinite period of time.

Article 694.—After dissolution of a partnership, the liquidation of its affairs is carried out either by all the partners jointly, or by liquidators appointed by them for that purpose.

The decision appointing the aforesaid liquidators shall be made by a majority vote of all the partners.

Article 695.—When there are several persons acting as liquidators, the decisions concerning the liquidation must be made by a majority vote.

Article 696.—In case one or more liquidators are appointed by the partnership contract from among the partners, the provisions of Article 674 are applicable.

Article 697.—The assets of the partnership must be first used for the payment of its debts.   If a debt has not

177

Chapter II   *Particular Kinds of Obligations*

THE CHINESE CIVIL CODE

yet matured or is the subject of litigation, the amount necessary for the performance of such debt shall be taken out from the assets of the partnership, and be reserved.

After all the debts have been paid or the necessary amounts for same have been taken out in accordance with the preceding paragraph, the contributions of the partners must be refunded from the remaining assets.

For the settlement of the debts and the return of the contributions, the property of the partnership shall, as far as necessary, be converted into money.

Article 698.—If the assets of the partnership are not sufficient for reimbursing the contributions, the reimbursement shall be made *pro rata,* in proportion to the respective value of each contribution.

Article 699.—If there is a balance of assets remaining, after the payment of the debts and the return of contributions, it shall be divided among the partners, in the proportion in which they are entitled to the profits.

Title XIX — Sleeping Partnership

ARTICLES 698 TO 706

TITLE XIX.—SLEEPING PARTNERSHIP

Article 700.—A contract of sleeping partnership is a contract whereby one of the parties agrees to furnish a contribution to an enterprise managed by the other party, on the understanding that the former will share in the profits and losses of the enterprise.

Article 701.—In addition to the provisions of this title, the provisions concerning Partnership apply *mutatis mutandis* to Sleeping Partnership.

Article 702.—On the contribution of the sleeping partner being handed over, the right over same passes to the active partner.

Article 703.—In respect to losses, the sleeping partner is liable only to the extent of his contribution.

Article 704.—The affairs of the sleeping partnership shall be exclusively managed by the active partner.

No rights or obligations towards third persons shall accrue to the sleeping partner on account of transactions entered into by the active partner.

Article 705.—If a sleeping partner takes part in the management of the affairs of a sleeping partnership or declares that he takes part in it or knowing that other persons declare that he is taking part in it, does not deny it, he becomes liable to third parties as an active partner, notwithstanding any agreement to the contrary.

Article 706.—Notwithstanding any agreement to the contrary, a sleeping partner may at the expiration of each business year, inspect the books of the partnership and

Chapter II	Particular Kinds of Obligations

THE CHINESE CIVIL CODE

make investigations as to its business and financial state.

For serious reasons, the Court may, on the application of a sleeping partner, authorise such sleeping partner to make, at any time, inspections or investigations as specified in the preceding paragraph.

Article 707.—Unless otherwise provided for by contract, the active partner shall, at the expiration of each business year, take stock and find out the profits and losses made, and pay immediately to the sleeping partner the profits accrued to him.

Unless otherwise agreed upon, profits which are accrued to the sleeping partner but have not yet been paid out cannot be considered as increases of his contribution.

Article 708.—In addition to the provisions of Article 686 by which a sleeping partner is entitled to declare his withdrawal, a sleeping partnership is terminated in any of the following cases:—

1. Expiration of the agreed time;
2. Consent of the parties;
3. Accomplishment of the enterprise or impossibility of accomplishing same;
4. Death or declaration of interdiction of the active partner;
5. Bankruptcy of the sleeping or active partner;
6. Cessation or transfer of enterprise.

Article 709.—In case of the termination of a sleeping partnership, the contribution of the sleeping partner must be returned by the active partner together with the profit accruing to him. However, if the contribution is decreased by losses, only the balance shall be returned.

TITLE XX.—ORDERS OF PAYMENT

Article 710.—An order of payment is a document whereby a person directs another person to deliver to a third person money or valuable securities or other fungible things.

Under the preceding paragraph, the person who directs is called the drawer; the person who is directed is called the drawee; and the person to whom presentation is made is called the payee.

Article 711.—When the drawee has notified the payee that he accepts to execute the order of payment, he is bound to execute it in accordance with the tenor of the order.

In the case specified in the preceding paragraph, the drawee may set up against the payee only such defences as arise from the tenor of the order or from his legal relations with the payee.

Article 712.—If an order of payment is made by the drawer for the performance of a debt due to the payee, the debt is extinguished when prestation is made by the drawee.

In the case specified in the preceding paragraph, the creditor who has accepted an order of payment cannot claim payment of the original debt from the drawer, unless he has been unable to procure execution of the order by the drawee within the time specified in the order, or, if no time is specified, within a reasonable time.

A creditor who is not willing to accept an order of

Chapter II   *Particular Kinds of Obligations*

THE CHINESE CIVIL CODE

payment from his debtor must notify the latter of his refusal without delay.

Article 713.—Even though the drawee is indebted to the drawer, he is not bound to accept the order of payment nor to execute it. If he executes it, he is released from his debt to the drawer to the amount of his performance.

Article 714.—If the drawee refuses acceptance or execution of the order of payment, the payee must notify the drawer of the refusal without delay.

Article 715.—A drawer may revoke his order of payment so long as the drawee has not notified the payee of his acceptance or execution of the order. Such revocation shall be made by a declaration of intention to the drawee.

The order is deemed to be revoked, if the drawer is declared a bankrupt before the acceptance or execution of the order by the drawee.

Article 716.—The payee may transfer the order to a third person, unless the drawer has inserted in the order itself that transfer is forbidden.

The transfer specified in the preceding paragraph must be made by endorsement.

If the drawee accepts the order in favour of the transferee, he cannot set up against the latter defences resulting from his legal relations with the payee.

Article 717.—The claim of the payee or the transferee against the drawee who has accepted the order of payment is extinguished by prescription, if not exercised within three years from date of acceptance.

Title XX   *Orders of Payment*

ARTICLES 713 TO 718

Article 718.—In case an order has been lost, stolen or destroyed, the Court may, on the application of the bearer, declare the order invalid by means of proceedings by public summons.

Chapter II   *Particular Kinds of Obligations*

The Chinese Civil Code

Title XXI.—Obligations to Bearer

Article 719.—An obligation to bearer is an instrument by which the bearer may claim from the maker a prestation according to the tenor thereof.

Article 720.—The maker of an obligation to bearer is bound to make the prestation to the person who presents it. However, he cannot make such prestation if he knows that the bearer is not entitled to dispose of the instrument, or if he has been notified of the loss, theft or destruction of the same.

The maker is released from his obligation if he has performed according to the provisions of the preceding paragraph, even if the bearer was not entitled to dispose of the instrument.

Article 721.—The maker of an obligation to bearer is bound by it towards *bonâ fide* bearers, even if it has been stolen from him, or lost by him, or has otherwise passed into circulation without his consent.

An obligation to bearer does not lose its effect, even if the instrument is issued after the maker has died or has become incapable of disposing.

Article 722.—The maker of an obligation to bearer may set up against the bearer only the defences which result from the invalidity of the instrument itself, or from its tenor, or from his legal relations with the bearer.

Article 723.—The bearer of an obligation to bearer is bound to surrender the instrument to the maker on his requesting performance.

Title XXI   *Obligations to Bearer*

ARTICLES 719 TO 726

When the maker has, in accordance with the provisions of the preceding paragraph, received back the said instrument, he acquires the ownership of same, even if the bearer was not entitled to dispose of it.

Article 724.—If an obligation to bearer is damaged or defaced in such a way as to be no more fit for circulation, but its essential contents and distinctive marks are still recognizable, the bearer is entitled to request the maker to issue a new obligation on surrender of the old one.

The costs of replacement are to be borne by the bearer, except in the case of banknotes or other currency notes, where the costs are to be borne by the maker.

Article 725.—In case an obligation to bearer has been lost, stolen or destroyed, the Court may, on the application of the bearer, declare the instrument invalid by means of proceedings by public summons.

In the case provided for in the preceding paragraph, the maker is bound to give the bearer such information concerning the obligation as may be necessary for proceeding by public summons, and to supply him with whatever evidence that is necessary.

Article 726.—When a period for the presentation of an obligation to bearer has been fixed, if the Court has, on the application of a person taking proceedings by public summons, ordered the stoppage of payment by the maker, the period of presentation is suspended.

The suspension provided for in the preceding paragraph runs from the time of the application for the

Chapter II *Particular Kinds of Obligations*

THE CHINESE CIVIL CODE

aforementioned order, and ends on the termination of the proceedings by public summons.

Article 727.—When the maker of obligations to bearer has been notified of the loss, theft or destruction of coupons for interest, annuity or dividends, if such coupons are not presented for payment before the expiration of the period of prescription provided by law for periodical payments, the bearer who made the notification is entitled to claim from the maker the payment of the interest, annuity or dividends accruing to the said coupons. However, this claim shall be extinguished by prescription after one year from the date of expiration of the prescription period.

If, before the expiration of the prescription period, the coupons are presented for payment by a third party, the maker shall notify the third party that payment has been stopped and shall defer payment until such third party and the person making the notification have come to an agreement, or until the case has been decided by a final judgment of a competent Court.

Article 728.—The provisions of the last sentence of paragraph 1, Article 720, and of Article 725 do not apply to obligations to bearer which bear no interest but are payable at sight, except coupons for interest, annuity and dividends.

Title XXII   *Life Interests*

ARTICLES 727 TO 735

TITLE XXII.—LIFE INTERESTS

Article 729.—A contract of life interest is a contract whereby the parties agree that one of them shall make periodical payments in money to the other party or to a third person, during the lifetime of one or the other of the parties or of a third person.

Article 730.—A contract of life interest must be made in writing.

Article 731.—In a contract of life interest, where there is a doubt as to its duration, the life interest is presumed to be payable to the creditor during his lifetime.

In case of doubt, the amount mentioned in the contract is presumed to be the amount to be paid annually.

Article 732.—Unless otherwise provided in the contract, a life interest is payable quarterly in advance.

If the person, on whose life the life interest depends, dies after a payment made in advance and before the expiration of the period for which the payment was made, the creditor is entitled to the whole amount advanced for that period.

Article 733.—When the death which terminated the life interest is due to circumstances for which the debtor of the life interest is responsible, the Court may, on the application of the creditor or of his heirs, decide that the life interest shall continue for a reasonable period of time.

Article 734.—Unless otherwise provided for by contract, the right to a life interest cannot be transferred.

Article 735.—The provisions of the present title apply *mutatis mutandis* to the legacy of life interests.

Chapter II   *Particular Kinds of Obligations*

THE CHINESE CIVIL CODE

TITLE XXIII.—COMPROMISE

Article 736.—A compromise is a contract whereby the parties by making mutual concessions terminate an existing dispute or prevent the occurrence of a future dispute.

Article 737.—The effect of a compromise is to extinguish the rights abandoned by each party and to secure to each party those rights which are specified in the compromise.

Article 738.—A compromise cannot be avoided for mistake, except in any of the following cases:—

1. If the compromise is based on documents which are afterwards discovered to be forged or altered, provided that the forgery or alteration be such that the party concerned would not have agreed to compromise if he had known of the forgery or alteration.

2. If the object of the compromise had been settled by a final judgment of the Court, of which the parties or one of them had no knowledge at the time of the compromise.

3. If one of the parties was acting under a mistake as to the qualification of the other party or as to the point in dispute, which was essential in the case.

Title XXIV   *Suretyship*

Articles 736 to 745

Title XXIV.—Suretyship

Article 739.—A suretyship is a contract whereby the parties agree that one of them shall be bound to satisfy an obligation, when the debtor of the other party fails to perform same.

Article 740.—Unless otherwise provided for by contract, the suretyship shall include the interest on the principal debt, the penalty, the compensation for damages, and other accessory charges.

Article 741.—In case the liability of the surety is heavier than that of the principal debtor, it shall be reduced to the level of the principal debt.

Article 742.—The surety is entitled to set up any defence that is open to the principal debtor.

He can still set up such defences even if they are waived by the principal debtor.

Article 743.—A suretyship given for an obligation which is invalid on account of mistake or want of disposing capacity is still valid, if the surety binds himself in spite of the knowledge of the fact.

Article 744.—If the principal debtor has the right of cancelling the juristic act upon which the debt is founded, the surety is entitled to refuse to satisfy the obligation.

Article 745.—A surety may refuse performance to the creditor, so long as the creditor has not filed proceedings for compulsory execution, against the property of the principal debtor, without results.

Chapter II   *Particular Kinds of Obligations*

THE CHINESE CIVIL CODE

Article 746.—The surety cannot assert the right specified in the preceding article in any of the following cases:—

1. If the surety has waived his rights specified in the preceding article.

2. If, after the conclusion of the contract of suretyship, claims for performance against the principal debtor have become difficult on account of his having changed his domicile or his industrial or commercial location or his residence.

3. If the principal debtor has been declared bankrupt.

4. If the property of the principal debtor is not sufficient to satisfy the creditor.

Article 747.—A claim for performance and acts which interrupt prescription made against the principal debtor operate against the surety.

Article 748.—Unless otherwise agreed upon, when several persons act as sureties for one and the same debt, they are joint sureties for the said debt.

Article 749.—After the surety has satisfied the creditor, the claim of the creditor against the principal debtor is transferred to the surety to the extent of the performance.

Article 750.—If the surety has assumed the suretyship by reason of a mandate of the principal debtor, the surety may request the principal debtor to procure his discharge from the suretyship under any of the following cases:—

Title XXIV   *Suretyship*

ARTICLES 746 TO 753

1. If the property of the principal debtor has obviously decreased.

2. If, after the conclusion of the contract of suretyship, claims for performance against the principal debtor have become difficult on account of his having changed his domicile, or his industrial or commercial location or his residence.

3. If the principal debtor is in default.

4. If the creditor has obtained a judgment entitling him to compel the surety to perform.

If the principal obligation is not yet due, the principal debtor may give security to the surety instead of procuring his discharge.

Article 751.—If the creditor waives a real right on which his claim is secured, the surety is released from his obligation to the extent of the rights which have been waived.

Article 752.—If the suretyship has been given for a definite period of time, the surety is released from his obligation, if within such period the creditor fails to enter judicial proceedings against the surety.

Article 753.—If the suretyship is given for an indefinite period of time, the surety may, after the maturity of the principal debt, fix a reasonable period of not less than one month and request the creditor to enter judicial proceedings against the principal debtor within such period.

If the creditor fails to enter judicial proceedings against the principal debtor within the period specified

Chapter II   *Particular Kinds of Obligations*

THE CHINESE CIVIL CODE

in the preceding paragraph, the surety is released from his obligation.

Article 754.—If suretyship is given for a series of obligations and for an indefinite period of time, the surety may at any time terminate the contract by giving notice to the creditor.

In the case of the preceding paragraph, the surety is not liable for the obligations incurred by the principal debtor after the notice has reached the creditor.

Article 755.—If suretyship has been given for an obligation which is to be performed at a definite time and the creditor grants to the principal debtor an extension of time, the surety is released from his obligation, unless he has agreed to the extension.

Article 756.—A person who gives a mandate to another to open credit to a third party in the name and on the account of such other person is liable to the mandatory as a surety for the obligation of the third party arising from the opening of the credit.

BOOK III

RIGHTS OVER THINGS

CHAPTER I.

GENERAL PROVISIONS

Article 757.—No rights over things can be created other than those provided for by the present Code or by other laws.

Article 758.—Rights over immovables, which are acquired, created, lost and altered according to juristic acts, are not effective until registration has taken place.

Article 759.—A person, who has acquired rights over immovables by succession, compulsory execution, expropriation or a judgment of the Court before registration, cannot dispose of such rights until registration has taken place.

Article 760.—The transfer or creation of rights over immovables must be made in writing.

Article 761.—The transfer of rights over a movable is effective only by the delivery of the movable. However, if the transferee has been in possession of the movable, the transfer takes effect when the parties agree to such transfer.

In the transfer of a right over a movable, where the transferor is still in possession of it, a contract causing the transferee to acquire its indirect possession may be concluded between the parties in the place of a delivery.

Chapter I   *General Provisions*

The Chinese Civil Code

In the transfer of a right over a movable, where a third party is in possession of it, the transferor, may, in the place of a delivery, transfer to the transferee the claim against such third person for the return of the said movable.

Article 762.—If the ownership of, and any other right over one and the same thing belong to one and the same person, such other right is extinguished by merger, unless the owner or a third party has a legal interest in the continuance of such other right.

Article 763.—If any right over a thing other than ownership, and another right whose object is the said right over the thing belong to one and the same person, such other right is extinguished by merger.

The proviso in the preceding article applies *mutatis mutandis* to the case of the preceding paragraph.

Article 764.—Unless otherwise provided for by law, rights over things are extinguished by waiver.

Chapter II

—

OWNERSHIP

Title I.—General Provisions

Article 765.—The owner of a thing has the right, within the limits of the law or ordinances, to use it, to receive its benefits, and to dispose of it freely, and to exclude others from interfering with it.

Article 766.—Unless otherwise provided for by law, the component parts of a thing and the natural fruits thereof, belong, even after their separation, to the owner of the thing.

Article 767—The owner of a thing has the right to demand it back from anyone, who possesses it without authority or who seizes it. If his ownership is impaired, or when it is feared that such ownership will be impaired, the owner can demand the removal or the prevention of such impairment.

Article 768.—A person who has, with the intention of being an owner, enjoyed for five years the open and peaceful possession of a moveable of another, acquires its ownership.

Article 769.—A person who has, with the intention of being an owner, enjoyed continuously for twenty years

Chapter II   *Ownership*

THE CHINESE CIVIL CODE

the peaceful possession of an immovable of another, which has not been registered, can claim to be registered as the owner of the said immovable.

Article 770.—Where a person has, with the intention of being an owner, enjoyed continuously for ten years the peaceful possession of an immovable of another which has not been registered and the said possession is, at its beginning, *bonâ fide* and without any fault, such person can claim to be registered as the owner of the said immovable.

Article 771.—Where the possessor has voluntarily interrupted his possession or where his possession has become one without the intention of ownership, or where he has been deprived of such possession by another person, the prescription to acquire the ownership is interrupted, unless his possession is restored according to the provisions of Article 949 or 962.

Article 772.—The provisions of the preceding four articles apply *mutatis mutandis* to the acquisition of rights over property other than ownership.

Title II   *Ownership of Immovables*

ARTICLES 770 TO 777

TITLE II.—OWNERSHIP OF IMMOVABLES

Article 773.—Unless restricted by law or by ordinances, ownership of land extends to such height and depth above and below the surface as is advantageous for the exercise of such ownership. Interference by others cannot be excluded if it does not obstruct the exercise of the ownership.

Article 774.—In carrying on an industry and in exercising other rights, the owner of a piece of land shall take care to prevent the occurrence of any injury to the adjacent land.

Article 775.—The owner of a lower land cannot prevent the natural flow of water coming from a higher land.

Water which flows naturally from a higher land and is necessary to the lower land cannot be wholly prevented or obstructed by the owner of the higher land, even if it is indispensable to the higher land.

Article 776.—When, owing to the disruption or obstruction of works constructed on a piece of land for the purposes of collecting, drawing or conducting water, damage has been caused or it is feared that damage will be caused to land belonging to another, the owner of the land must, at his own expenses make such repairs or drain off the water or take preventive measures, as may be necessary. However, if the bearing of such expenses is otherwise provided for by custom, such custom shall be followed.

Article 777.—The owner of a piece of land cannot

Chapter II   *Ownership*

THE CHINESE CIVIL CODE

construct a roof or other structures which will cause rain water to fall directly upon adjacent immovable property.

Article 778.—When the course of water on a lower piece of land is obstructed by accident, the owner of the higher land may construct necessary works for its drainage at his own expenses. However, if the bearing of such expenses is otherwise provided for by custom, such custom shall be followed.

Article 779.—For the purposes of draining marshy land or discharging superfluous water from a household or from agricultural or industrial uses, the owner of the higher land may conduct such water through the lower land until it reaches a drain or public water-way, provided that the place and method of conducting the course of water shall be so chosen as will cause the least injury to the lower land.

In the case of the preceding paragraph, the owner of the higher land must make compensation for any injury caused to the lower land.

Article 780.—The owner of a piece of land may, for the purposes of conducting water on his land, use the works constructed by the owner of the higher or lower piece of land, but he must pay his share of the expenses for the construction and maintenance of such works in proportion to the benefit which he derives therefrom.

Article 781.—The owner of a land where water originates, or of a well, drain or other ground through which water flows, may freely use the water, unless there is a special custom.

Title II   *Ownership of Immovables*

ARTICLES 778 TO 785

Article 782.—The owner of a land where water originates, or of a well, can claim damages against a person, who, owing to the works carried on by him, cuts off, reduces or pollutes the water from such land or well. If the water is indispensable for drinking or for utilizing the land, the said owner may claim to have the *status quo ante* restored, unless restoration is impossible.

Article 783.—The owner of a land, who cannot procure the water indispensable for his household or for utilizing his land without undertaking excessive expenses or labour, is entitled on paying a compensation to demand from the owner of the adjacent land such part of his own water as exceeds his needs.

Article 784.—The owner of a land on which water flows cannot change the course of the water or its width, when the land on the opposite shore belongs to another person.

When the land on both shores belongs to the owner of the land on which water flows, he can change the course of the water or its width, provided the water shall be restored to its natural course at its lower mouth.

In the case of the two preceding paragraphs, if it is otherwise provided for by custom, such custom shall be followed.

Article 785.—The owner of land through which water flows may, when it is necessary to construct a dam, rest the dam on the opposite shore, provided that a compensation shall be made for any injury resulting therefrom.

The owner of the opposite shore may use the dam

Chapter II   *Ownership*

THE CHINESE CIVIL CODE

specified in the preceding paragraph, when a part of the land through which water flows belongs to him, provided that he shall bear a share of the expenses of construction and maintenance of such dam in proportion to the benefits which he derives therefrom.

In the case of the two preceding paragraphs, if it is otherwise provided for by custom, such custom shall be followed.

Article 786.—Where electric wires, water pipes, gas pipes or other pipes cannot be constructed without making use of the land of another or where they can only be constructed through the incurring of excessive expenses, the owner of a piece of land may construct the said wires or pipes on, over or under the ground of another person, provided that the place and method of constructing such wires or pipes are so chosen as will cause the least injury to such other person and provided that a compensation is paid.

If, after the construction of electric wires, water pipes, gas or other pipes has been made in accordance with the provisions of the preceding paragraph, the circumstances have changed, the owner of the other land is entitled to demand that the aforesaid construction be changed.

The cost of the alteration of such construction shall be borne by the owner who constructs. But if it is otherwise provided for by custom, such custom shall be followed.

Article 787.—If, in the absence of suitable access to the public road, a piece of land is not fit for ordinary use, the owner of the land is entitled to a right of passage

Title II   *Ownership of Immovables*

ARTICLES 786 TO 790

over the surrounding land in order to reach the public road, provided that a compensation shall be made for any injury caused thereby to the land passed over.

In the case of the preceding paragraph, the place and methods of passage must be so chosen as to meet the needs of the person entitled to the right of passage and at the same time to cause the least injury to the surrounding land.

Article 788.—The person entitled to the right of passage may construct a road when necessary, but he must pay a compensation for any injury caused thereby to the land through which the road passes.

Article 789.—If, in consequence of a transfer of a part of a piece of land or of a partition of a piece of land, one of the partitioned parts has no access to the public road, the owner of such partitioned part is entitled to a right of passage to the public road only through the land owned by the transferee or the transferor or the other participants.

In the case specified in the preceding paragraph, the person entitled to the right of passage is not liable to pay a compensation.

Article 790.—The owner of a piece of land has the right to prohibit other persons from tresspassing on his land. But this does not apply to any of the following cases:—

1. When there is a right of passage on the land.

2. When, according to local custom, it is allowed to enter his (the owner's) field, pasture or forest, around

Chapter II   *Ownership*

THE CHINESE CIVIL CODE

which no fence has been made, for the purpose of cutting grass, of gathering dead branches or timber, of collecting wild products or of feeding cattle.

Article 791.—If things or animals have by accident entered another person's land, the owner of the land must allow the owner or possessor of the things or animals to enter the land in order to recover them and take them back.

In the case specified in the preceding paragraph, the owner of the land is entitled to claim compensation for damage, if any; and he can also retain the said things or animals until such compensation has been paid.

Article 792.—The owner of a piece of land must allow the owner of an adjacent land to use such part of his land as may be necessary for the construction or repair of structures which are on or near the boundary line. But he can claim compensation for any damage resulting therefrom.

Article 793.—The owner of a piece of land may prohibit the discharge of gases, steam, bad odours, smoke, heat, soot, noises, vibrations and other similar nuisances proceeding from another person's land, unless such nuisance is insignificant or is justified by the respective locations of the two pieces of land or by local custom.

Article 794.—In making excavations or in erecting buildings, the owner of the land must not cause the foundations of the adjacent land to be shaken or endangered, nor can he cause any injury to the structures of the adjacent land.

204

Title II   *Ownership of Immovables*

ARTICLES 791 TO 799

Article 795.—If a piece of land is threatened with the danger of being damaged by the falling of the whole or a part of a building or other structures on the adjacent land, the owner of the land is entitled to claim that necessary measures for the prevention of such danger be taken by the owner of the adjacent land.

Article 796.—If the owner of a piece of land builds a house beyond the boundary, the owner of the adjacent land, who knows of the trespass and does not immediately object to it, cannot claim the removal or alteration of the structure; but he is entitled to claim that the builder must buy that part of the land trespassed upon at a reasonable price and to claim damages for additional injury, if any.

Article 797.—If the branches or roots of bamboos or trees of the adjacent land spread beyond the boundary, the owner of the land has the right to require the owner of the bamboos or trees to cut down the said branches and roots within a reasonable time.

If the owner of the bamboos or trees does not cut down the said branches or roots within the time specified in the preceding paragraph, the owner of the land may cut and keep the encroaching branches or roots.

The provisions of the two preceding paragraphs do not apply to such encroaching branches or roots that will not interfere with the utility of the land.

Article 798.—Fruits that fall naturally on a neighbouring land are deemed to belong to such land, unless it is a public land.

Article 799.—When a building is partitioned by

Chapter II *Ownership*

The Chinese Civil Code

several persons, and each of them owns a part of it, the part in common use of the building and its accessories is presumed to be jointly owned by all the owners. The costs of repairs to the building and other charges shall be borne by all the owners in proportion to the value of their own respective parts.

Article 800.—In the case of the preceding article, if it is necessary for the owner of a part of the building to make use of the middle gate which belongs to another owner, he is entitled to do so; but if it is otherwise provided for by a special agreement or custom, such agreement or custom shall be followed.

Compensation shall be made for any injury caused to the owner through such use as specified in the preceding paragraph.

Title III   *Ownership of Movables*

ARTICLES 800 TO 806

TITLE III.—OWNERSHIP OF MOVABLES

Article 801.—When a transferee of a movable is put in possession of it and is protected by the provisions concerning Possession, he acquires the ownership of same even if the transferor has no right to transfer such ownership.

Article 802.—Whoever with the intention of being the owner of a movable which has no owner takes possession of the same acquires its ownership.

Articles 803.—A person who finds a thing that is lost is bound to inform its owner. If the owner is unknown, or if there is nothing to show where the owner is, the finder shall either advertise the find or inform the police or the local autonomous institution and deposit it with them at the time of such information.

Article 804.—If, after the find has been advertised, its owner does not appear within a reasonable time, the finder shall inform the competent police authorities or the local autonomous institution and deposit it with them.

Article 805.—If the owner appears within six months from the date of the finding, the finder or the police authorities or the local autonomous institution shall return him the find after he (the owner) has reimbursed them with the costs of advertising and of keeping it.

In the case specified in the preceding paragraph, the finder is entitled to claim from the owner a remuneration equivalent to three-tenths of the value of the find.

Articles 806.—If the find is of a such nature that it will easily perish, or if its preservation would cost

Chapter II	Ownership

THE CHINESE CIVIL CODE

disproportionate expenses, the police authorities or local autonomous institution may sell it by auction and keep the net proceeds of the sale.

Article 807.—If the owner does not appear within one year from the date of the finding, the police authorities or local autonomous institution shall deliver the find or the net proceeds of its sale by auction to the finder, who shall become the owner of same.

Article 808.—Whoever discovers a treasure-trove and takes possession of it acquires its ownership. But, if the treasure-trove is discovered in a movable or immovable owned by another, the discoverer and the owner of such movable or immovable shall each acquire a half of the treasure-trove.

Article 809.—When a treasure-trove that has been discovered possesses a scientific, artistic, archaeological or historic value, its ownership shall be determined in accordance with the provisions of the special law relating thereto.

Article 810.—The provisions concerning the finding of lost things apply to the finding of flotsam or articles sunk.

Article 811.—When a movable becomes an important component part of an immovable through joining, the owner of the immovable acquires the ownership of such movable.

Article 812.—When a movable belonging to one person is joined to another movable belonging to another person in such a way that they cannot be separated

Title III   *Ownership of Movables*

ARTICLES 807 TO 816

without damage or can only be separated through the incurring of excessive expenses, both owners shall jointly own the new product proportionately to the value of each movable at the time they were joined.

If one of the movables joined as specified in the preceding paragraph can be deemed to be the principal thing, the owner of such principal thing acquires the ownership of the new product.

Article 813.—The provisions of the preceding article apply *mutatis mutandis* when a movable is mixed together with a movable belonging to another person so as to be no longer distinguishable from each other or when it can only be distinguished through the incurring of excessive expenses.

Article 814.—When a person has contributed work to a movable belonging to another, the ownership of the movable upon which the work is done belongs to the owner of the material thereof; but, if the value of the workmanship obviously exceeds the value of the material, the ownership of the movable upon which the work is done belongs to the workman.

Article 815.—When the ownership of a movable is extinguished in accordance with the provisions of the four preceding articles, all other rights over such movable are also extinguished.

Article 816.—A person who has suffered injury by loss of rights through the provisions of the preceding five articles, is entitled to claim a compensation in accordance with the provisions concerning Undue Enrichment.

Chapter II   *Ownership*

THE CHINESE CIVIL CODE

TITLE IV.—CO-OWNERSHIP

Article 817.—When several persons have the owner-ship of a thing in proportion to their own respective shares, they are co-owners.

If the shares to which each co-owner is entitled are not known, it is presumed that such shares are equal.

Article 818.—Each co-owner is, in proportion to his own share, entitled to use the whole of the joint property and to collect its fruits.

Article 819.—Each co-owner may freely dispose of his own share.

The disposition of, the alteration of and the creation of an encumbrance over a joint property can only be made with the consent of all the co-owners.

Article 820.—Unless otherwise provided for by con-tract, the joint property shall be administered by the co-owners in common.

In regard to simple repairs and such other acts for the preservation of the joint property, each of the co-owners can act alone.

Improvements on the joint property can only be carried out with the consent of the majority of the co-owners, whose own shares *in toto* represent a greater portion of the property.

Article 821.—Each co-owner may exercise against third parties for the whole of the joint property, the rights resulting from ownership. But a claim for restoration of the said property can only be made for the common benefit of all the co-owners.

Title IV   *Co-Ownership*

ARTICLES 817 TO 824

Article 822.—Unless otherwise provided for by contract, the costs of administration and other charges relating to the joint property are to be borne by all the co-owners in proportion to their respective shares.

When one of the co-owners has paid more than the share incumbent on him for the charges relating to such joint property he is entitled to claim a reimbursement from the other co-owners in proportion to their respective shares.

Article 823.—Each co-owner is entitled to demand at any time the partition of the joint property. However, this does not apply if, in consequence of the object of using such property, partition is impossible, or if it is provided for by contract that no partition can be made within a certain period.

The period for non-partition fixed by such contract as mentioned in the preceding paragraph cannot exceed five years; where a period exceeding five years has been agreed upon, it shall be reduced to five years.

Article 824.—The partition of the joint property shall be made in the method mutually agreed upon between the co-owners.

If the method of partition cannot be mutually agreed upon, the Court may, on the application of any of the co-owners, order such partition to be made according to either of the following:—

1. The distribution of the property itself among the co-owners, or

2. The sale of the property and the distribution of the net proceeds among the co-owners.

In the case of the distribution of the property itself,

Chapter II   *Ownership*

THE CHINESE CIVIL CODE

if some of the co-owners cannot obtain their allotted parts in proportion to their own shares, they can be further compensated in money.

Article 825.—Each co-owner in proportion to his share bears a liability or warranty similar to that of a seller in regard to the things which the other co-owners have acquired by partition.

Article 826.—After the partition of a joint property, each participant shall preserve all documents relating to the thing which he has acquired.

After the partition of a joint property, all documents relating to the said property shall be preserved by the person who has acquired the largest portion of the thing. If no person has acquired a larger portion, the participants shall by mutual agreement determine who shall preserve the said documents; and if it cannot be determined by mutual agreement, he shall be nominated by the Court on the application of the participants.

Each participant is entitled to claim the use of the documents preserved by the other participants.

Article 827.—Where, according to the provisions of law or according to a contract, several persons are joined in a community, by virtue of which they jointly own the same property, such persons are owners-in-common.

The rights of each owner-in-common extend to the whole property in common.

Article 828.—The rights and duties of the owners-in-common are determined according to the law or contract which provides for the community.

Title IV   *Co-Ownership*

ARTICLES 825 TO 831

Unless otherwise provided for by law or contract as specified in the preceding paragraph, the disposition of the property in common and the exercise of other rights relating to the same must be made with the consent of all the owners-in-common.

Article 829.—During the continuance of the community, no owner-in-common can demand the partition of the property in common.

Article 830.—The ownership-in-common is extinguished with the termination of the community or by the transfer of the property in common.

Unless otherwise provided for by law, the methods relating to the partition of the property in common shall be in accordance with the provisions governing the methods relating to the partition of joint property.

Article 831.—The provisions of this title apply *mutatis mutandis,* when rights over property other than ownership belong to several co-owners or owners-in-common.

Chapter III.

SUPERFICIES

Article 832.—Superficies is the right to use the land of another person with the object of owning thereon structures or other works or bamboos or trees.

Article 833.—The provisions of Articles 774 to 798 apply *mutatis mutandis* between superficiaries or between superficiary and landowner.

Article 834.—If the period of the superficies has not been fixed, the superficiary can at any time waive his right unless otherwise provided for by custom.

The waiver of the superficies as specified in the preceding paragraph shall be made by a declaration of intention to the landowner.

Article 835.—Where the rent for superficies has been agreed upon, and where the superficiary waives his right, either one year's previous notice shall be given to the landowner, or rent for the following year shall be paid.

Article 836.—Where payment of the rent has been delayed by the superficiary and the accumulated amount in arrears is equivalent to the total rent for two years, the landowner is entitled to revoke the superficies, unless otherwise provided for by custom.

The revocation as specified in the preceding paragraph

Chapter III   *Superficies*

The Chinese Civil Code

shall be made by a declaration of intention to the superficiary.

Article 837.—The superficiary is not entitled to claim for a release or reduction of the rent even if he is hindered by *force majeure* from using the land.

Article 838.—The superficiary may transfer his rights to another person, unless it is otherwise provided for by contract or by custom.

Article 839.—When the superficies is extinguished, the superficiary can remove his works and bamboos and trees provided that the *status quo ante* of the land shall be restored.

In the case specified in the preceding paragraph, if the landowner wishes to purchase such work or bamboos and trees at their current market price, the superficiary cannot refuse to sell.

Article 840.—Where the work of the superficiary is a building and the superficies is extinguished through the expiration of the duration of the contract, the landowner must reimburse him according to the current price of such building.   But if it is otherwise provided for by contract, such provisions shall be followed.

Before the expiration of the duration of the superficies, the landowner can ask the superficiary to prolong the duration of the superficies to such period as the building may be used.   If the superficiary refuses, he cannot claim a reimbursement as specified in the preceding paragraph.

Article 841.—A superficies is not extinguished by the loss or destruction of the structures or bamboos or trees.

CHAPTER IV

———

YUNG-TIEN

Article 842.—Yung-tien is the right to cultivate or to raise live-stock permanently on the land of another person by paying a rent.

Where a yung-tien is created for a definite period of time, it is deemed to be a lease, and the provisions concerning Lease shall apply.

Article 843.—A yung-tien holder may transfer his right to another person.

Article 844.—A yung-tien holder is entitled to claim a reduction or a release of his rent, if, owing to *force majeure,* his profits have decreased or totally failed.

Article 845.—A yung-tien holder cannot lease the land to another person.

If a yung-tien holder acts contrary to the provision of the preceding paragraph, the landowner may revoke the yung-tien.

Article 846.—Where payment of the rent has been delayed by the yung-tien holder and the accumulated amount in arrears is equivalent to the total rent for two years, the landowner may revoke the yung-tien, unless otherwise provided for by custom.

Article 847.—The revocation specified in the two

Chapter IV   *Yung-tien*

The Chinese Civil Code

preceding articles shall be made by a declaration of intention to the yung-tien holder.

Article 848.—The provisions of Article 839 apply *mutatis mutandis* to Yung-tien.

Article 849.—Where the yung-tien holder has transferred his right to a third person, such third person is bound to repay to the landowner the rent owed by all previous yung-tien holders.

Article 850.—The provisions of Articles 774 to 798 apply *mutatis mutandis* between yung-tien holders, or between yung-tien holder and landowner.

CHAPTER V

——

SERVITUDES

Article 851.—Servitude is the right to use the land of one person for the convenience of the land of another person.

Article 852.—Servitudes cannot be acquired by prescription except those which are continuous and apparent.

Article 853.—A servitude may neither be transferred nor made the object of any other right by separating from the dominant land.

Article 854.—The owner of the dominant land is entitled to perform such acts as are necessary for the exercise or maintenance of his rights, but the place and method of exercising his rights must be so chosen as to cause the least injury to the servient land.

Article 855.—The owner of a dominant land, who makes constructions for the purpose of exercising his rights, is bound to maintain such constructions.

The owner of the servient land may use the constructions as specified in the preceding paragraph, except where it will obstruct the exercise of the servitude.

In the case specified in the preceding paragraph, the owner of the servient land shall bear his share of the

Chapter V *Servitudes*

The Chinese Civil Code

expenses for the maintenance of the constructions in proportion to the benefit he derives therefrom.

Article 856.—Where the dominant land is partitioned, its servitude still continues for the benefit of all its parts. But, if according to its nature the exercise of the servitude actually refers to one part only of the dominant land, such servitude will continue only in respect to such part.

Article 857.—Where the servient land is partitioned, the servitude still continues on all its parts. But, if according to its nature the exercise of the servitude actually refers to one part only of the servient land, such servitude will continue only as against such part.

Article 858.—The provisions of Article 767 apply *mutatis mutandis* to Servitudes.

Article 859.—Where the continuance of the servitude is no longer necessary, the Court may, on the application of the owner of the servient land, declare such servitude extinguished.

CHAPTER VI

———

MORTGAGE

Article 860.—Mortgage is the right to receive performance of an obligation from the proceeds of sale of the immovable which has been given as security for the obligation by the debtor or by a third person, without transferring its possession.

Article 861.—Unless otherwise provided for by contract, a mortgage secures the principal debt, its interest, interest for default, and cost of executing the mortgage.

Article 862.—The effect of a mortgage extends to the accessories and accessory rights of the property mortgaged.

Rights acquired by third parties over such accessories before the creation of the mortgage are not affected by the provisions of the preceding paragraph.

Article 863.—The effect of a mortgage extends to the natural fruits which have been separated from the property mortgaged after the seizure of such property.

Article 864.—The effect of a mortgage extends to the legal fruits which the mortgagor can collect from the property mortgaged after the seizure of such property. However, the mortgagee cannot oppose the payment of the legal fruits by the person bound to pay them, until

Chapter VI

THE CHINESE CIVIL CODE

he has notified such person of the fact of seizing the mortgaged property.

Article 865.—Where the owner of an immovable creates several mortgages on the same property for securing several obligations, the ranks of these mortgages are determined according to the priority of registration.

Article 866.—After the creation of the mortgage, the owner of an immovable may create on the same immovable superficies and other rights, but the mortgage is not affected thereby.

Article 867.—After the creation of the mortgage, the owner of an immovable can transfer the said immovable to another person, but the mortgage is not affected thereby.

Article 868.—When an immovable mortgaged has been partitioned or partially transferred, or when one of the several immovables securing the same claim is transferred to another person, the mortgage is not affected thereby.

Article 869.—Where a claim secured by a mortgage has been partitioned or partially transferred, the mortgage is not affected thereby.

The provision of the preceding paragraph applies to the case where a debt is partitioned.

Article 870.—A mortgage may neither be transferred nor made the security for any other claim by separating it from the claim.

Article 871.—Where the act of the mortgagor is

Mortgage

ARTICLES 865 TO 874

likely to cause the value of the property mortgaged to depreciate, the mortgagee can claim an injunction to stop such act; and, in an urgent case, the mortgagee himself can take the necessary measures to safeguard the mortgage.

Costs incurred for such injunction or measures as specified in the preceding paragraph shall be borne by the mortgagor.

Article 872.—Where the value of the property mortgaged has depreciated, the mortgagee can demand that the mortgagor shall restore the *status quo ante* of the said property, or give security corresponding to the value depreciated.

Where, owing to circumstances for which the mortgagor is not responsible, the value of the property mortgaged has depreciated, the mortgagee can demand security to be given for any damages only to such an extent as the mortgagor can be compensated for the said damage.

Article 873.—The mortgagee, who has not been paid at the maturity of an obligation in his favour, can apply to the Court to have the mortgaged property sold by auction and to pay himself out of the proceeds of the sale.

Any agreement which provides that, if the obligation is not fulfilled at its maturity, the ownership of the mortgaged property shall pass and belong to the mortgagee, is void.

Article 874.—The amount from the sale of the

Chapter VI

THE CHINESE CIVIL CODE

mortgaged property shall be distributed to the mortgagees according to their rank of priority. In case they are of the same rank, such amount shall be distributed *pro rata*.

Article 875.—If a mortgage has been created on several immovables for the security of one and the same claim without specifying the amount to be charged against each of the said immovables, the mortgagee can demand performance of the whole or a part of his claim from the proceeds of the sale of each of the said immovables.

Article 876.—Where a piece of land and any building thereon belong to one and the same person and either the land or the building only is mortgaged, the super-ficies is deemed to have been created at the time when the property mortgaged is sold by auction. Its rent, however, shall be determined by mutual agreement between the parties; and, if such an agreement cannot be reached, it shall be fixed by the Court upon application.

Where a piece of land and any building thereon belong to one and the same person and both the land and the building are mortgaged, if the land and the building are sold to different bidders at an auction, the provisions of the preceding paragraph shall apply.

Article 877.—If, after the creation of a mortgage, the landowner erects structures on the land mortgaged, the mortgagee may when necessary have the structures sold by auction together with the land, but he shall not have any preferential right to receive performance from the proceeds of the sale of such structures.

Mortgage

ARTICLES 875 TO 883

Article 878.—After the maturity of his claim has expired, a mortgagee may, in order to satisfy himself, acquire by agreement the ownership of the property mortgaged, or dispose of the same by any means other than an auction, unless it is prejudicial to the interest of the other mortgagees.

Article 879.—When a third person, who creates a mortgage for a debtor, pays the debt in full for such debtor, or loses the ownership over the property mortgaged through the execution of the mortgage by the mortgagee, such third person is entitled to a right of recourse against the said debtor according to the provisions governing Suretyship.

Article 880.—In an obligation secured by mortgage, where its right of claim has been extinguished by prescription, the mortgage is extinguished if not exercised by the mortgagee within five years after the completion of such prescription.

Article 881.—A mortgage is extinguished through the loss of the property mortgaged, but the compensation which could be received from such loss shall be distributed to the mortgagees according to their rank of priority.

Article 882.—Superficies, yung-tien and dien may be the object of a mortgage.

Article 883.—The provisions of the present chapter concerning Mortgage apply *mutatis mutandis* to the mortgage specified in the preceding article and to statutory mortgage.

Chapter VII

PLEDGE

Title I.—Pledge of Movables

Article 884.—Pledge of movables is the right to take possession of the movable delivered by the debtor or a third party as security for an obligation and to receive performance of the said obligation from the proceeds of sale of that movable.

Article 885.—The creation of a pledge becomes effective by the delivery of the possession of the thing pledged.

The pledgee cannot cause the pledgor to possess in his place the thing pledged.

Article 886.—The pledgee, who takes possession of the movable and is protected under the provisions concerning Possession, acquires the pledge even if the pledgor is not entitled to dispose of the thing pledged.

Article 887.—Unless otherwise provided for by contract, a pledge secures the principal debt, its interest, interest in default, the cost of executing the pledge and any damages arising from a concealed defect in the thing pledged.

Article 888.—The pledgee must keep the thing pledged with the care of a good administrator.

| Chapter VII | Pledge |

THE CHINESE CIVIL CODE

Article 889.—The pledgee is entitled to collect the fruits produced from the thing pledged, unless otherwise provided for by contract.

Article 890.—The pledgee, who has the right to collect the fruits from the thing pledged, shall collect such fruits with the same care as he would have taken for his own and shall render an account.

The fruits as specified in the preceding paragraph shall first meet the costs of collecting the fruits, then the interest on the principal debt, and finally, the principal debt.

Article 891.—During the continuance of the pledge, the pledgee may, on his responsibility, sub-pledge the thing pledged to a third person. He is also responsible for any loss or damage caused by *force majeure* resulting from the sub-pledge.

Article 892.—Where it is feared that the thing pledged will perish or where its value obviously depreciates to a point sufficient to endanger the rights of the pledgee, he may sell the thing pledged by auction and keep the proceeds thereof in the place of the thing pledged.

Article 893.—The pledgee who has not been paid at the maturity of an obligation in his favour can sell the thing pledged by auction and pay himself out of the proceeds of the sale.

Any agreement, which provides that if the obligation is not fulfilled at its maturity the ownership of the thing pledged shall pass and belong to the pledgee, is void.

Article 894.—In the case of the two preceding

Title I *Pledge of Movables*

ARTICLES 889 TO 899

articles the pledgee shall notify the pledgor before the sale by auction, unless such notification is impracticable.

Article 895.—The provisions of Article 878 concerning Mortgage apply *mutatis mutandis* to Pledge of Movables.

Article 896.—Upon the extinction of the obligation secured by the pledge of a movable, the creditor shall return the thing pledged to the person entitled to receive it.

Article 897.—The pledge of a movable is extinguished through the return of the thing pledged by the pledgee to the pledgor.

Upon the return of the thing pledged, any reservation made in regard to the continuance of the pledge is void.

Article 898.—A pledge of a movable is extinguished, when the pledgee loses possession of the thing pledged and cannot demand the return of it.

Article 899.—The pledge of a movable is extinguished by the loss of the thing pledged. But if a compensation can be obtained for such loss, the pledgee is entitled to be paid out of the compensation.

Chapter VII   *Pledge*

THE CHINESE CIVIL CODE

TITLE II.—PLEDGE OF RIGHTS

Article 900.—A transferable claim and other rights may be the object of a pledge.

Article 901.—In addition to the provisions of this title, the provisions concerning Pledge of Movables apply *mutatis mutandis* to Pledge of Rights.

Article 902.—Unless provided for in the present title, the creation of a pledge of rights shall be made in accordance with the provisions applicable to the transfer of such rights.

Article 903.—The pledgor cannot, by means of a juristic act, cause the right which is the object of a pledge to be extinguished or modified without the consent of the pledgee.

Article 904.—Where the object of a pledge is a claim its creation shall be made in writing; and, if there is any document relating to the said claim, such document shall also be delivered to the pledgee.

Article 905.—Where an obligation which is the object of a pledge matures before the obligation secured by it is due, the pledgee can claim the thing delivered for the performance of the obligation pledged to be lodged by the debtor.

Article 906.—Where an obligation which is the object of a pledge matures after the obligation secured by it is due, the pledgee can, at the maturity of the former, claim performance directly from the debtor. However, if the obligation consists of money, he is only entitled

Title II   *Pledge of Rights*

ARTICLES 900 TO 910

to claim the payment of that amount, which corresponds to the amount of the obligation in his favour against the pledgor.

Article 907.—Where the object of a pledge is an obligation and its debtor has been notified of the creation of such pledge, he cannot make any performance either to the pledgor or to the pledgee without the consent of the other party. In the absence of such consent the debtor must lodge the thing delivered for the performance.

Article 908.—Where the object of a pledge consists of an instrument to bearer, the creation of the pledge becomes effective by the delivery of such instrument to the pledgee. In case the object consists of other valuable securities, an entry is also required to be made according to the rules of endorsement.

Article 909.—If the object of a pledge is an instrument to bearer, negotiable instrument or any other instrument which can be transferred by endorsement, the pledgee is, even if the obligation secured by it is not matured, entitled to collect the prestations accruing to him through such instrument, and, where previous notice is necessary to be given to the debtor of an instrument, he is entitled to make such notice; the debtor may make performance only to the pledgee.

Article 910.—Where the object of a pledge is a valuable security, the effect of such pledge extends to interest coupons, periodical payment coupons, or dividend coupons belonging thereto, provided they have been delivered to the pledgee.

Chapter VIII

—

DIEN

Article 911.—Dien is the right to use an immovable of another person and to collect fruits therefrom by paying a price and taking possession of the immovable.

Article 912.—The duration of a dien cannot exceed thirty years. If a period exceeding thirty years has been agreed upon, such period shall be reduced to thirty years.

Article 913.—Where a period of less than fifteen years has been agreed upon for the duration of the dien, no clause, which provides that if the property is not redeemed within such period it is considered sold without a right of redemption, is allowed to be included in the contract.

Article 914.—The provisions of Articles 774 to 800 apply *mutatis mutandis* between dien-holders or between dien-holder and landowner.

Article 915.—During the continuance of the dien, the dien-holder can sub-dien or lease the property diened to another person. But if it is otherwise agreed upon between the parties or if it is otherwise provided for by custom, such agreement or custom shall apply.

Where a period has been fixed for the duration of the dien, the period of the sub-dien or lease cannot exceed that of the original dien. In the absence of such fixed

Chapter VIII

THE CHINESE CIVIL CODE

duration, no definite period can be fixed for the sub-dien or lease.

The price for the sub-dien cannot exceed the price of the original dien.

Article 916.—The dien-holder is liable to make compensation for any injury caused to the property diened resulting from the sub-dien or lease.

Article 917.—The dien-holder can transfer the dien to another person.

In the case of the preceding paragraph, the transferee acquires the same rights as a dien-holder against the dien-maker.

Article 918.—The dien-maker may after the creation of the dien transfer the ownership of the property diened to another person.

The dien-holder is still entitled to the same rights as against the transferee specified in the preceding paragraph.

Article 919.—Where the dien-maker transfers the ownership of the property diened to another person, if the dien-holder expresses his desire to keep and to purchase the property at the same price, the dien-maker cannot refuse to sell without a justifiable reason.

Article 920.—If, during the continuance of the dien, the property diened has been wholly or partially lost by *force majeure,* both the dien and the right of redemption are extinguished in respect to the part lost.

In the case of the preceding paragraph, if the dien-holder redeems the part remaining, he may deduct from

Dien

ARTICLES 916 TO 924

the original price received for the dien a half of the value which the part lost had at the time of such loss, provided that the deduction shall not exceed the original price.

Article 921.—If, during the continuance of the dien, the property diened is wholly or partially lost by *force majeure,* the dien-holder can re-construct or repair the property diened only up to the value which the part lost had at the time of such loss, except with the consent of the dien-maker.

Article 922.—If, during the continuance of the dien, the property diened is wholly or partially lost through the fault of the dien-holder, he is liable for such loss up to the amount of the price given for the dien. However, if the loss is caused by his intentional acts or gross negligence, he shall make compensation for further injury, if any, in addition to that covered by the price given for the dien.

Article 923.—Where a period is fixed for the duration of the dien, the dien-maker is entitled to redeem the property diened at the original price after the expiration of such period.

If the dien-maker does not redeem the property diened at the original price within two years from the expiration of the aforementioned period, the dien-holder acquires the ownership of that property.

Article 924.—Where no period has been fixed for the duration of the dien, the dien-maker can redeem the property diened at any time at the original price. However, if it is not redeemed within thirty years from the

Chapter VIII *Dien*

THE CHINESE CIVIL CODE

creation of the dien, the dien-holder acquires the ownership of the property diened.

Article 925.—If the property diened is an agricultural land, the redemption by the dien-maker shall be made after the season when the crops are reaped and before the beginning of the next cultivation. If the property consists of any other immovable, the dien-holder must be notified six months beforehand.

Article 926.—If, during the continuance of the dien, the dien-maker expresses his desire to transfer to the dien-holder the ownership of the property diened, the dien-holder may acquire such ownership by paying the difference between the current value of the property diened and the price given for such dien.

The payment of the difference specified in the preceding paragraph shall be made once only.

Article 927.—Where beneficial expenses have been incurred by the dien-holder, whereby the value of the property diened is increased, or where reconstruction or repairs have been made in accordance with the provisions of Article 921, the dien-holder may claim reimbursement to the extent of the benefits existing at the time of the redemption of the said property.

CHAPTER IX

—

RIGHT OF RETENTION

Article 928.—Until his claim is satisfied, the creditor who is in possession of a movable belonging to his debtor, may retain the same on the fulfilment of all the following conditions:—

1. Where the obligation existing in his favour is matured,

2. Where there is a connection between the source of the obligation and the movable, and

3. Where the possession of the movable did not originate from a wrongful act.

Article 929.—The connection specified in the preceding article is deemed to exist, where the movable is taken into possession on account of business relations between traders and where the claim arises from such trade relation.

Article 930.—No retention over a movable can be made, if the retention is contrary to public order or good morals. The same rule applies where it is in conflict with the obligations assumed by the creditor or with the instructions given by the debtor before or at the delivery of the movable.

Article 931.—On the insolvency of the debtor, the

237

Chapter IX

THE CHINESE CIVIL CODE

creditor has the right of retention, even before the obligation becomes due.

Where the debtor becomes insolvent after the delivery of the movable or where his insolvency becomes known to the creditor after such delivery, the creditor is entitled to exercise his right of retention, even if it is in conflict with the obligation assumed by him or with the instructions of the debtor as specified in the preceding article.

Article 932.—The creditor may exercise his right of retention against the whole thing retained until the obligation in his favour is wholly performed.

Article 933.—The creditor must keep the thing retained with the care of a good administrator.

Article 934.—The creditor is entitled to claim reimbursement from the owner of the thing retained for any necessary expenses incurred for the custody of the said thing.

Article 935.—In order to satisfy his claim, the creditor is entitled to collect the fruits produced from the thing retained.

Article 936.—The creditor may, when the obligation in his favour is not performed at its maturity, fix a reasonable period of at least six months and notify the debtor that if the obligation is not performed within such period, he will satisfy himself out of the thing retained.

If the debtor does not perform within the period specified in the preceding paragraph, the creditor may, in accordance with the provisions concerning the execution of pledge, sell by auction the thing retained or acquire its ownership.

Right of Retention

ARTICLES 932 TO 939

Where the notification as specified in the first paragraph is impossible, the creditor can also exercise the right as specified in the preceding paragraph, if the obligation is not performed within two years from the expiration of its maturity.

Article 937.—If the debtor has given proper security for the performance of the obligation, the right of retention by the creditor is extinguished.

Article 938.—The right of retention over a thing is extinguished by the loss of its possession.

Article 939.—Unless otherwise provided for, the provisions of the present chapter apply *mutatis mutandis* to statutory retention.

CHAPTER X

POSSESSION

Article 940.—A possessor is a person who has a controlling power *de facto* over a thing.

Article 941.—Where a person possesses a thing of another as a pledgee, lessee, or depositary, or by virtue of some other similar legal relation, such other person is an indirect possessor.

Article 942.—Where, by following the instructions of another person, a person has the controlling power over a thing as an employee or apprentice, or by virtue of some other similar relation he is entitled to the said power, then only such other person is the possessor.

Article 943.—A possessor is presumed to have lawfully the right which he exercises over the thing possessed.

Article 944.—It is presumed that the possessor of a thing possesses it with the intention to become its owner, in good faith, peacefully and openly.

When it is proved that possession existed at the beginning and at the end of a period, it is presumed that the possessor has been in continuous possession during the intermediate time.

Article 945.—When, according to the nature of the facts from which the possession of a thing originates, the

Chapter X

THE CHINESE CIVIL CODE

possessor has no intention to become an owner of it, he takes the possession with the intention of being its owner from the time when he expresses such intention to the person who has put it in his possession. The same rules apply when the possession becomes one with the intention of ownership through a new fact.

Article 946.—The transfer of possession becomes effective by the delivery of the thing possessed.

The provisions of Article 761 apply *mutatis mutandis* to the transfer as specified in the preceding paragraph.

Article 947.—The successor or transferee in a possession may assert either his own possession or his possession together with that of his predecessor.

In case the possession of the predecessor is asserted together with that of his own, he succeeds also to its defects.

Article 948.—Where, with a view of transferring or creating the ownership of, or other rights over a movable, the possession of the same is assumed in good faith, such possession shall be protected by law even if the transferor had no right to deliver it.

Article 949.—If the thing possessed is a booty or something lost by another, the sufferer or the loser can demand from the possessor the restoration of the thing within two years from the time when the thing was stolen or lost.

Article 950.—Where the booty or the thing lost is bought in good faith by the possessor at a sale by auction, or in a public market, or from traders selling things

Possession

ARTICLES 946 TO 956

similar to the one possessed, the thing cannot be restored without reimbursing the buyer with the price he paid for it.

Article 951.—In case the booty or thing lost consists of moneys or instruments to bearer, restoration of the same cannot be claimed from its *bonâ fide* possessor.

Article 952.—A *bonâ fide* possessor can use the thing possessed and collect fruits therefrom in accordance with the right which is presumed to be lawfully had by him.

Article 953.—If, in consequence of circumstances for which the *bonâ fide* possessor is responsible the thing possessed is lost or injured, he is liable for damages to the person claiming the restoration only to the extent of the profits which he, the said possessor, has received by reason of the loss or injury.

Article 954.—A *bonâ fide* possessor can demand from the person claiming restoration reimbursement of any necessary expenses incurred for the custody of the thing possessed. However, he cannot claim such reimbursement, if he has collected the fruits of the said thing.

Article 955.—A *bonâ fide* possessor can demand from the person claiming restoration reimbursement for any beneficial expenses incurred for the improvement of the thing possessed in so far as the existing value of the thing is increased thereby.

Article 956.—If, owing to circumstances for which a *mala fide* possessor or anyone possessing the thing without the intention of being its owner is responsible,

Chapter X

THE CHINESE CIVIL CODE

the thing possessed is lost or injured, he is liable to the person claiming restoration for any damages arising therefrom.

Article 957.—A *mala fide* possessor can demand from the person claiming restoration reimbursement for any necessary expenses incurred for the preservation and protection of the thing possessed in accordance with the provisions concerning Management of Affairs Without Mandate.

Article 958.—A *mala fide* possessor is liable for the return of fruits. If the fruits have been consumed, or have been injured through his own fault, or have not been collected through his neglect, he is bound to make compensation for the value of such fruits.

Article 959.—A *bonâ fide* possessor, who fails in a petitory action, shall be deemed as a *mala fide* possessor from the date at which the pendency of the action comes into force.

Article 960.—A possessor can defend himself with his own force against any act which deprives him of or interferes with his possession.

Where the thing possessed has been dispossessed, the possessor can, if it is an immovable, regain the same by expelling the wrongdoer immediately after the dispossession; or, if it is a movable, regain it from the wrongdoer in the very act or in a pursuit.

Article 961.—The person entitled to the controlling power as specified in Article 942 may also exercise the right of the possessor provided for in the preceding article.

Possession

ARTICLES 957 TO 966

Article 962.—Where possession has been taken away from a possessor, he can claim the return of the thing taken; where it is interfered with, he can claim the removal of the interference; and where it is feared that it will be interfered with, he can claim the prevention of such interference.

Article 963.—The right of claim as specified in the preceding article is existinguished by prescription, if not exercised within one year from the time of the dispossession or interference or from the existence of the fear of being interfered with.

Article 964.—The possession of a thing is extinguished by the loss of the controlling power *de facto* which the possessor exercises over the said thing, unless the non-exercise of such controlling power is only temporary.

Article 965.—If several persons possess a thing in common, no claim for the protection of possession can be made against one another in so far as the limits of using the said thing are concerned.

Article 966.—A quasi-possessor is a person who exercises such property rights over a thing as are established without having taken possession of the said thing.

The provisions of the present chapter concerning Possession apply *mutatis mutandis* to the quasi-possession as specified in the preceding paragraph.

LAW GOVERNING THE APPLICATION

of

THE GENERAL PRINCIPLES OF THE

CIVIL CODE

LAW GOVERNING THE APPLICATION

OF THE

GENERAL PRINCIPLES OF
THE CIVIL CODE

Article 1.—Unless otherwise provided for by the present Law of Application, the provisions of the General Principles of the Civil Code are not applicable to civil matters that occurred before the coming into force of the General Principles of the Civil Code.

Article 2.—Within the limits prescribed by law or ordinances, a foreigner has the capacity of enjoying rights.

Article 3.—The provisions of Articles 8, 9 and 11 of the General Principles of the Civil Code are also applicable to cases where the disappearance of a person occurred before the coming into force of the General Principles of the Civil Code.

At the time when the General Principles come into force, a person who has disappeared for a longer period than that provided in Article 8 of the General Principles of the Civil Code, may be declared dead. And the date of the coming into force of the General Principles shall be the date of death of such missing person.

Article 4.—If, before the coming into force of the General Principles of the Civil Code, a person had been registered with the competent authorities for causes (feeblemindedness) provided in Article 14 of the General

Law Governing the Application of Book I

Principles of the Civil Code, and has been duly interdicted by the Court within three months from the coming into force of the General Principles of the Civil Code, he is considered an interdicted person as from the date of registration.

Article 5.—A juristic person, who should be authorised in accordance with the provisions of the General Principles of the Civil Code and to whom authorisation has been granted by the competent authorities before the coming into force of the General Principles, may apply for registration as a juristic person within three months from the date of the coming into force of the General Principles of the Civil Code.

Article 6.—A foundation which came into existence before the coming into force of the General Principles of the Civil Code and whose object is for the promotion of public welfare and which possesses independent property, is regarded as a juristic person. Its representatives (directors) must apply, in accordance with the provisions of Article 47 or 60 of the General Principles of the Civil Code, prepare a petition and have it presented to the competent authorities within the six months from the date of the coming into force of the General Principles of the Civil Code, for inspection and approval.

If any of the matters in the petition mentioned in the foregoing paragraph is, in the opinion of the competent authorities, contrary to law and ordinances, or is against public interest, the competent authorities shall order modification.

The petition approved as in the first paragraph has the same effect as a constitution.

General Principles

Article 7.—The representatives (directors) of a juristic person, whose petition as provided in the preceding article has been approved by the competent authorities, shall apply for registration within twenty days of such approval in accordance with the provisions of Article 48 or 61 of the General Principles of the Civil Code.

Article 8.—If the juristic person as defined in Article 6 has not prepared an inventory of the property and a register of its membership, it shall do so immediately after the coming into force of the General Principles of the Civil Code.

Article 9.—The provisions of Articles 6 to 8 are not applicable to ancestral halls, monasteries and temples and those independent properties used for the purposes of maintaining a family.

Article 10.—In the registration of a juristic person, as provided in the General Principles of the Civil Code, the competent authorities are the Court of the place where the office of the juristic person is situated.

The Court shall immediately promulgate those matters that have already been registered and permit any third person to copy or read same.

Article 11.—No foreign juristic person shall be allowed to come into existence except in accordance with the provisions of law.

Article 12.—Within the limits prescribed by law and ordinances, a recognized juristic person has the same capacity of enjoying rights as a Chinese juristic person.

In the observation of Chinese Law a foreign juristic person mentioned in the foregoing paragraph is under the same obligations as a Chinese juristic person.

Law Governing the Application of Book I

Article 13.—The provisions of Articles 30, 31, 45, 46, 48, 59, 61 and of the preceding article apply *mutatis mutandis* to a foreign juristic person which has established offices within the territory of China.

Article 14.—If the office of a foreign juristic person established in accordance with the provisions of the preceding article is found to carry on those activities mentioned in Article 36 of the General Principles of the Civil Code, the Court may avoid them.

Article 15.—When a person enters upon a juristic act with others in the name of an unrecognized foreign juristic person, the doer is jointly liable along with the foreign juristic person for such juristic act.

Article 16.—If, before the coming into force of the General Principles of the Civil Code, extinctive prescription is already completed in accordance with the provisions of the General Principles of the Civil Code, or the remainder of the period of prescription is less than one year, the right of claim may be enforced within one year from the date of the coming into force (of the General Principles of the Civil Code).

But this does not apply when the time, beginning from the completion of the prescription to the coming into force of the General Principles of the Civil Code, exceeds half of the period of prescription as provided in the General Principles of the Civil Code.

Article 17.—The provisions of the preceding article are applicable *mutatis mutandis* to the right of avoidance provided in paragraph 2 of Article 74, Articles 90 and 93.

Article 18.—If a statutory extinctive prescription is

General Principles

already completed before the coming into force of the General Principles of the Civil Code, the prescription is deemed to be completed.

If the statutory period of extinctive prescription, before the coming into force of the General Principles of the Civil Code, is longer than that fixed by the General Principles of the Civil Code, the old law shall apply. But if the remainder of the period, reckoning from the date of the coming into force of the General Principles of the Civil Code, is longer than the period of prescription fixed by the General Principles of the Civil Code, the General Principles of the Civil Code shall apply as from the date of their coming into force.

Article 19.—The present Law of Application comes into force as from the date of the coming into force of the General Principles of the Civil Code.

LAW GOVERNING THE APPLICATION

of

THE BOOK OF OBLIGATIONS OF THE CIVIL CODE

LAW GOVERNING THE APPLICATION

OF THE

BOOK OF OBLIGATIONS OF
THE CIVIL CODE

Article 1.—Unless otherwise provided for by the present Law of Application, the provisions of the Book of Obligations of the Civil Code are not applicable to obligations that occurred before the coming into force of the Book of Obligations of the Civil Code.

Article 2.—If, before the coming into force of the Book of Obligations, the period of extinctive prescription is already completed in accordance with the provisions of the Book of Obligations of the Civil Code, or the remainder of the period of prescription be less than one year, the right of claim may be enforced within one year from the date of its coming into force. This does not apply when the time, beginning from the completion of the prescription to the coming into force of the Book of Obligations of the Civil Code, exceeds half of the period of prescription as provided in the Book of Obligations of the Civil Code.

If, in accordance with the provisions of the Book of Obligations, the period of extinctive prescription is less than one year and the period is not yet completed before the coming into force of the Book of Obligations, the prescription is reckoned from the date of its coming into force.

Law Governing the Application of Book II

Article 3.—The provisions of the preceding article apply *mutatis mutandis* to the statutory period of non-prescriptive nature as provided in the Book of Obligations of the Civil Code.

Article 4.—The provisions of Article 204 apply *mutatis mutandis* to rates of interest exceeding 12% per annum which were agreed upon before the coming into force of the Book of Obligations.

Article 5.—The provisions of the Book of Obligations of the Civil Code are also applicable to the fixing up of the amount of an obligation incurred before the coming into force of the Book of Obligations of the Civil Code and which has not been performed at the time. But if, at the time when the Book of Obligations comes into force, the total amount of unpaid interest exceeds the principal, the total amount of interest shall be made not to exceed the principal.

Article 6.—The provisions of Articles 217 and 218 apply *mutatis mutandis* to obligations to make compensation for injury done before the coming into force of the Book of Obligations of the Civil Code.

Article 7.—When an obligation incurred before the coming into force of the Book of Obligations of the Civil Code is not performed after its coming into force, the debtor is responsible for non-performance in accordance with the provisions of the Book of Obligations of the Civil Code.

The provisions of the foregoing paragraph apply *mutatis mutandis,* when the creditor refuses or fails to accept performance.

Obligations

Article 8.—The provisions of Articles 250 to 253 apply to penalty which was agreed upon before the coming into force of the Book of Obligations of the Civil Code.

Article 9.—On the publicly certified acknowledgment mentioned in Article 308 made by the creditor, the Court, notary, police authorities, chamber of commerce, or local autonomous institution of the place of performance shall be requested to affix his or their seal and signature.

Article 10.—The provisions of Article 318 apply *mutatis mutandis* to an obligation incurred before the coming into force of the Book of Obligations of the Civil Code.

Article 11.—Obligations incurred before the coming into force of the Book of Obligations of the Civil Code may also be discharged by off-set in accordance with the provisions of the Book of Obligations of the Civil Code.

Article 12.—In a contract of redemption concluded before the coming into force of the Book of Obligations of the Civil Code, if the redemption period is fixed, such period shall be followed. But if the remainder of the period, reckoning from the date of the coming into force (of the Book of Obligations of the Civil Code) is longer than that provided for in Article 380 of the Civil Code, provisions of Article 380 shall apply as from the date of their coming into force. In the event where no definite period is provided for in the contract of redemption, the period shall not exceed five years, beginning from the date of the coming into force (of the Book of Obligations of the Civil Code).

Law Governing the Application of Book II

Article 13.—The validity of a lease agreement which was made before the coming into force of the Book of Obligations of the Civil Code shall be in accordance with the provisions of the Book of Obligations of the Civil Code.

If the period of the lease mentioned in the foregoing paragraph is fixed in the agreement, such period shall be followed. But if the remainder of the period, reckoning from the date of the coming into force (of the Book of Obligations of the Civil Code) is longer than that provided for in Article 449 of the Civil Code, the provisions of Article 449 shall apply as from the date of their coming into force.

Article 14.—Before the promulgation of the Law of Auction Sale, the auction as provided in the Book of Obligations of the Civil Code may be sold according to market value. But it must be certified by the Court, the notary, the police authorities, the chamber of commerce or the local autonomous institution.

Article 15.—The present Law of Application comes into force as from the date of the coming into force of the Book of Obligations of the Civil Code.

LAW GOVERNING THE APPLICATION

of the

BOOK OF RIGHTS OVER THINGS OF

THE CIVIL CODE

LAW GOVERNING THE APPLICATION

OF THE

BOOK OF RIGHTS OVER THINGS
OF THE CIVIL CODE

Article 1.—Unless otherwise provided for by the present Law of Application, the provisions of the Book of Rights over Things are not applicable to rights over things that existed before the coming into force of the Book of Rights over Things of the Civil Code.

Article 2.—Rights over things as provided in the Book of Rights over Things of the Civil Code which existed before the coming into force (of the Book of Rights over Things) become effective in accordance with the provisions of the Book of Rights over Things of the Civil Code, as from the date of their coming into force.

Article 3.—Concerning registration as provided in the Book of Rights over Things of the Civil Code, it shall be regulated by special law.

The provisions of the Book of Rights over Things of the Civil Code concerning registration are not applicable to rights over things that have not been registered in accordance with special law mentioned in the foregoing paragraph.

Article 4.—If, before the coming into force of the Book of Rights over Things of the Civil Code, extinctive prescription is already completed in accordance with the

Law Governing the Application of Book III

provisions of the Book of Rights over Things of the Civil Code, or the remainder of the period of prescription is less than one year, the right of claim may be enforced within one year from the date of the coming into force (of the Book of Rights over Things). But this does not apply when the time, reckoning from the completion of the prescription to the coming into force of the Book of Rights over Things of the Civil Code, exceeds half of the period of prescription as provided in the Book of Rights over Things of the Civil Code.

Article 5.—If, before the coming into force of the Book of Rights over Things of the Civil Code, the statutory period of non-prescriptive nature is completed, the period is deemed to be completed.

If, before the coming into force of the Book of Rights over Things of the Civil Code, the period has commenced to run, and the statutory period of non-prescriptive nature, as provided in the Book of Rights over Things of the Civil Code, is not yet completed at the time of the coming into force (of the Book of Rights over Things), the period that has already run shall be reckoned together with the period after the coming into force (of the Book of Rights over Things).

The provisions of the foregoing paragraph apply *mutatis mutandis* to acquisitive prescription.

Article 6.—A person who possessed a movable before the coming into force of the Book of Rights over Things of the Civil Code, and fulfils the conditions mentioned in Article 768, acquires its ownership as from the date of the coming into force (of the Book of Rights over Things) of the Code.

Rights over Things

Article 7.—A person who possessed an immovable before the coming into force of the Book of Rights over Things of the Civil Code and fulfils the conditions mentioned in Article 769 or 770, can claim as from the date of the coming into force (of the Book of Rights over Things) to be registered as the owner (of the said immovable).

Article 8.—A person, who can claim to be registered in accordance with law as the owner while the office of registration as provided in paragraph 1 of Article 3 (of the present Law of Application) is not yet established, may be considered as the owner as from the date when he applies for registration.

Article 9.—A person who possessed a movable before the coming into force of the Book of Rights over Things of the Civil Code and fulfils the conditions of Article 801 or 886, acquires its ownership or pledge as from the date of the coming into force (of the Book of Rights over Things).

Article 10.—A person who found lost things, flotsam, or articles sunk before the coming into force of the Book of Rights over Things of the Civil Code and fulfils the conditions of Articles 803 and 807, acquires the rights as provided in Article 807 of the Civil Code, as from the date of the coming into force (of the Book of Rights over Things).

Article 11.—If, before the coming into force of the Book of Rights over Things of the Civil Code, a person can acquire the ownership (of a thing) in accordance with the provisions of Article 808 or Articles 811 to 814

Law Governing the Application of Book III

of the Civil Code, he acquires the ownership as from the date of their coming into force.

Article 12.—If, in a contract specifying a period for the non-partition of a joint property concluded before the coming into force of the Book of Rights over Things of the Civil Code, the remainder of the period, reckoning from the date of its coming into force, is shorter than that provided for in paragraph 2 of Article 823, such period shall be followed. If it is longer, the provisions of paragraph 2 of Article 823 shall apply as from the date of their coming into force.

Article 13.—When a claim secured by a mortgage is extinguished by prescription in accordance with the provisions of the Civil Code before the coming into force of the Book of Rights over Things of the Civil Code, the period for the extinction of the mortgage, as provided in Article 880, is reckoned from the date of its coming into force. But if the time, reckoning from the completion of the extinctive prescription of the claim to the date of the coming into force (of the Book of Rights over Things), exceeds 10 years, the mortgage cannot be enforced.

Article 14.—The provisions of the Book of Rights over Things of the Civil Code concerning pledge are not applicable to pawnshops and others accepting things for pledge as business.

Article 15.—If, before the coming into force of the Book of Rights over Things of the Civil Code, a period is fixed for the duration of a dien and it may be redeemed according to the old rules of law, such old rules shall be followed.

Rights over Things

Article 16.—The present Law of Application comes into force as from the date of the coming into force of the Book of Rights over Things of the Civil Code.

INDEX

Index

THE REFERENCES ARE TO ARTICLES

A

Accessories—Definition, 68; prescription, 146; disposal, 68; transfer, 295, 304; extinction, 307; rescission of contract, 362, redemption, 383; lease of agricultural implements, 462, 463; building owned in common, 799; mortgage, 862.

Accessory charges, 740.

Accounts of partnership, 676; see also Current account.

Acknowledgment of claim—Interruption of prescription, 129; prescription and contractual acknowledgment of liability, 144.

Acknowledgment, public — Extinction of obligation, 308.

Acquisitive prescription—see Prescription.

Act of endowment—Foundation, 60.

Action—129, 130, 131, 137, 229, 534, 555, 558, 604.

Action, petitory, 959.

Acts, juristic—Nullity of, 71-73; voidability of, 74; disposing capacity, 75-85; contracts of person incapable of disposing, 79-82; agent's authority derived from, 105; entered in the name of principal, 106; without authority, 110, 170, 171; void, 111-113; voidable, 114, 116; ratification, 115, 116; validity dependent upon consent of third party, 117; dates and periods, 119-123; period of prescription not extendable by, 147; conferring of authority of agency by, 167; creation of rights over immovables, 758; extinction or modification of pledge by, 903; see also Contract, Declaration of intention.

Acts, wrongful—Definition, 184; joint-doers, 185; by officials, 186; by person without disposing capacity, 187; by employee, 188; by contractor, 189; by animal, 190; defective construction, 191; responsibility for funeral expenses, 192; resulting to loss of earning capacity, 193; indemnification, 18, 194, 195; value of thing, 196; prescription, 197, 198; infringement of personality, 18;

271

Index

infringement of name, 19; legitimate defence, 149, 150; undue enrichment, 180; right of retention, 928.

Administrator of property, 140; see also Directors.

Age—Calculation of, 124; majority, 12; minority, 13; acquisition of necessaries of life, 77.

Agency—Management of affairs of juristic person, power of agent, 27, 48, 61; declaration of intention by agent, 103; disposing capacity of agent, 104; defective intention and authority of agent, 105; limitation of power of agent, 106, 107, 557, 558; termination and revocation of power, 108, 109; absence of authority, 110, 170, 171, 544; conferring of authority, 167; plural, 168, 556; tacit authority, 169, 553; debtor responsible for acts of agent, 224; mandate, 531-534; manager, 553-555, 557; commercial agent, 558, 564; partnership, 679, 680.

Agent, statutory—Person incapable of disposing, 76-85; domicile of person incapable of disposing, 21; liability for wrongful acts of person incapable of disposing, 187; prescription against, 141; prescription between person incapable of disposing and his statutory agent, 142; extinction of mandate, 551.

Agricultural land—Lease, 457-463; yungtien, 842-850; dien, 925.

Amalgamation of several enterprises—306.

Animal—Natural fruit, 69; damage caused by, 190; leased, 418; leased as livestock, 462; 463; cost of provender by borrower, 469; owner of pasture, 790; enter another person's land by accident, 791; yungtien, 842.

Approval—Sale on, 384-387.

Arbitration—Authority of mandatory, 534.

Assignees—138; see also Heirs.

Association—Acquisition of juristic personality, 45; for promoting public welfare, 46; constitution, 47; contributions, registration, 48; organization, 49; general meeting, 50-53; withdrawal of members, 54-55; nullification of resolutions, 56; dissolution of, 57, 58.

Assumption of debt—300-306.

Attachment—340, 604, 685, 863, 864.

Attorneys—Prescription of remuneration of, 127.

Auction—Regulations, 391-397; lodgment, 331, 333; commission agent, 585; warehouseman, 621; carrier, 650-652, 656; perishable find, 806, 807; mortgage, 873, 876, 877; pledge, 892-894; *bonâ fide* booty, 950.

Index

Author—see Publication.

Authorities—see Competent authorities.

B

Bad faith (*Mala fide*)—175, 956-959.

Balance of current account—402.

Banknotes—724.

Bankruptcy—juristic person, 35; proceeding interrupt prescription, 129, 134; declaration, 140; termination of mandate, 550; of principal and authority of manager, 564; termination of partnership, 687, 708; principal debtor and surety, 746.

Bearer—see Obligations to bearer.

Bill of exchange — c u r r e n t account, 401.

Bill of lading—625, 627-630, 642, 649, 664.

Birth—6.

Bonâ fide—Third party, 27, 87, 92, 107, 110, 165, 294, 557, 721; possessor, 770, 944, 948, 950-955.

Brokerage—Definition, 565; remuneration, 566, 568, 570-572; duties of broker, 567; reimbursements, 569, 571; matrimonial, 573; not to disclose names, 575.

Branches of bamboos or trees of adjacent land—797.

Business—Authorized by person with limited disposing capacity, 85; relations, 929.

C

Cancellation—see Voidable, Null and void.

Capacity, legal — Duration, 6; cannot be waived, 16; juristic persons, 26.

Capacity, disposing—Minor, 13; interdiction, 14, 15; cannot be waived, 16; juristic person, 26; effect on declaration of intention by persons whose disposing capacity is impaired, 95; author, 527; mandate, 550; authority of manager upon principal's losing disposing capacity, 564; partnership, 687, 708.

Capacity, without disposing — Minor under seven years of age, 13; interdiction, 14, 15; domicile, 21; declaration of intention by person without disposing capacity, 75; statutory agent, 76; prescription, 141, 142; wrongful acts, 187; responsibility of debtor without disposing capacity, 221; broker and person without disposing capacity, 567; surety, 743.

Capacity, limited disposing — Minor, 13; domicile, 21; declaration of intention, 77, 96;

Index

juristic act, 78, 83; contract, 79-82; disposition of property, 84; carrying on business, 85; effect on declaration of intention by person becoming, 95; agent, 104-108; prescription, 141, 142; wrongful acts, 187; responsibility of debtor with, 221; broker and person with, 567; surety, 743.

Capital—Tendered payment, 323; presumed payment, 325.

Carriage—Definition of carrier, 622; prescription of cost of transportation, 127; claim for damages, 623; way-bill, 624; bill of lading, 625, 630; documents of information concerning goods, 626; facts concerning carriage determined by bill of lading, 627; delivery of bill of lading as transfer of ownership of goods, 629; dangerous goods, 631; delay in transportation, 632, 633; duties and liabilities of carrier, 634-641, 649, 659; goods transported by successive carriers, 637, 646, 653; transportation stopped, 642; notifying consignee on arrival, 643; consignee acquiring rights, 644; freight, 645, 646; right of retention, 647; acceptance of goods by consignee, 648; sale of unclaimed goods or luggage, 650-652, 656; carriage of passengers, 654; luggage, 655-658; passing of risks to buyer on delivery, 374; transportation

and buyer, 374, 376, 378, see also Forwarding agency.

Chamber of commerce—358.

Characters (writing)—4, 5.

Charges and taxes on lease—427.

Cheque—Current account, 401.

Child—7.

Choice (obligations) — 208-212; prestation impossible, 247.

Choice of prestation — 208-217; when one of prestations being impossible, 211-247.

Collusion—87, 571.

Commercial agent — Definition, 558; authority, 558; duties, 559; remuneration and reimbursement, 560; termination, 561-564; prohibited business, 562, 563; see also Agency.

Commercial custom—88.

Commission — Definition, 576; provisions of mandate applicable, 577; rights and duties of commission agent, 578; price of sale, 580, 581; remuneration and charges, 582; custody, 583, 584; to sell goods when not accepted, 585, 586; commission agent as seller or buyer, 587, 588; provisions of commission agents applicable to forwarding agency, 660; see also Forwarding agency.

Common — see Ownership - in - common.

Companies — see Limited companies.

274

Index

Compensation (reimbursement) —176, 192, 194, 213, 225, 226, 240, 259, 328, 375, 382, 445, 456, 463, 740; see also Damages.

Competent authorities—30, 32-34, 36, 46, 48, 59, 61, 65, 151, 358.

Compromise — Definition, 736; effects, 737; avoidance, 738; prescription interrupted by, 129, 133; through mandatory, 534.

Condition — Precedent and subsequent, 99; fulfilment of, 100, 101; prestation impossible, 246; sale on approval, 384; contract concluded through broker, 568; set-off, 335; see also Former or prior condition.

Constitution—Juristic person, 37, 44; association, 47-50, 53-56.

Construction (structure)—Damage caused by defective, 191; defect in, 484, 499-501, 506, 513; compensation for damaging adjacent property, 792; foundations of adjacent land, 794; threatened danger to adjacent land, 795; of a house trespassing beyond boundary, 796; owner-in-common, 799, 800; superficies, 832, 839-841; mortgage, 876, 877.

Contract — Formation of, 153; offer and acceptance, 154-163; form of, 166; entered by person limited in disposing capacity, 79-82; for impossible prestation, 246, 247, 266; earnest money, 248, 249; penalty and non-performance, 250-253; rescission

of, 255-263; counter-performance, 264-267; performance by third party, 268; performance to third person, 269, 270.

Contract for third person—269, 270, 341.

Contractor—see Hire of work.

Contribution of members of association—47, 48, 55.

Contribution — Partnership, 667-669; 673, 677, 689, 697, 698; sleeping partnership, 700, 702, 707, 709.

Co-ownership—Definition, 817; rights, 818, 819; administration, 820; costs of administration, 822; partition, 823-826; movable joining, 812; see also Ownership-in-common.

Coupon—see Interest.

Court—Ascertaining characters and figures in contract, 45; missing person, 8; interdiction, 14; wrongful acts to person or name, 18, 19; juristic person, 35, 36, 38, 39, 42, 43; associations, 51, 56, 58; foundations, 62-64; cancellation of juristic act or reduction of prestation, 74; non-essential points of agreement, 153; wrongful acts of person without disposing capacity, 187; wrongful acts of employee, 188; author of injury, 193; reducing damages when injured party also at fault, 217, 218; compulsory execution, 227; gratuitous act being prejudicial to creditor, 244; penalty, 251,

Index

252; delayed performance, 318; lodgment, 327, 331, 332; lease, 447; publication, 518, 527; brokerage, 572; sleeping partnership, 706; order of payment, 718; obligations to bearer, 725-727; life interest, 733; co-ownership, 824, 826; servitudes, 859; mortgage, 873, 876.

Creditor—In default, 234; of joint obligation, 271, 273, 283, 287, 291; indivisible prestation, 292, 293; transfer of obligations, 294.

Currency—Payment, 201; foreign, 202; loan, 480; deposit, 603; notes, 724; see also Money.

Current account—Definition, 400; periodic balance, 402, 403; interests, 404; cancellation or correction of an entry elapsed after one year, 405.

Custom—Application, 1, 2; special trade custom concerning accessories, 68; place of payment, 314; delivery of object sold and payment of price, 369; deduction of weight of packing, 372; cost of sale, 378; auction, 391; repairs by lessor, 429; payment of rent, 439; termination of lease, 450; remuneration for service, 483, 486, 488; remuneration for execution of work, 491; mandatory commissioning a third person, 537; remuneration of commercial agent, 560; remuneration of broker, 566, 570; commission, 579, 582; deposit, 592, 632; drain of water, 776,

778; use of water, 781; flowing of water, 784; dam, 785; laying wires and pipes, 786; trespass, 790; nuisances, 793; building owned-in-common, 800; superficies, 834, 836, 838; yungtien, 846; dien, 915.

D

Dam—785.

Damages—Extent, 216-218, 638, 640; non-performance, 225, 227; surety, 740; pledge, 887; cases where damages liable, 18, 19, 28, 35, 91, 110, 113, 114, 149, 150, 152, 165, 174, 176, 182, 184-197, 214, 225-228, 231-233, 247, 250, 260, 268, 327, 336, 358, 376, 383, 411, 432, 433, 434, 437, 444, 466, 468, 476, 489, 495, 506, 509, 511, 542, 544, 546, 549, 563, 591, 593, 596, 605-611, 631, 634-639, 641, 642, 649, 654, 658, 659, 661, 776, 779, 785-788, 791, 792, 796, 800, 816, 887, 891, 922, 956; cases where damages not liable, 149, 150, 151, 175, 328.

Dates and periods—Calculation, 119-124; missing person, 8; performance, 229, 236, 318; release of surety, 755; calling of general meeting, 51; nullification of resolution of general meeting, 56; cancellation of juristic act, 74; ratification of juristic act, 80; avoidance of declaration of intention, 90, 93;

Index

prescription uninterrupted, 130, 135, 139-143; acceptance of offer, 157-159, 161, 162; transfer of assets and liabilities, joint liabilities, 305; sale and time for delivery, 370; period for striking balance of current account, 402; correction of current account, 405; redemption period, 380; acceptance by buyer of thing on approval, 386, 387; return of thing by borrower, 478; discovery of defects in works and structures, 498-501; notifying proprietor of guest's loss or injury, 610; warehouseman, 619; acceptance of order of payment, 712; presentation of obligation to bearer, 726; notifying carrier of loss or injury, 648; transportation of goods, 632; take delivery of luggage, 658; exercise of right by mortgagee, 880; non-partition contract, 823; redemption of property by dien-maker, 923, 924; satisfaction of debt out of thing retained, 936.

Dead—Declared, 8, 9, 10.

Death— 6; presumption of, 8, 9, 11; effect on declaration of intention, 95; caused by wrongful act, compensation, 192, 194; of donor, 412, 415, 417; of donee, 415, 420; of lessee, 452; of borrower, 472; of contractor, 572; of author, 527; of one of parties in mandate, 550; of principal and authority of man-

ager, 564; of partner, 687; of active partner, 708; of maker of obligation, 721; life interest, 732, 733.

Debt—Assumption of, see Assumption of debt.

Debtor—Responsibility of, 220; without disposing capacity, 221; responsible for acts of his agent, 224; relieved from obligation, 225; failing to perform, 227; in default, 229; of joint obligation, 272, 274, 275, 280, 282; indivisible prestation, 292, 293; and transfer of claim, 299.

Declaration of intention — Of person incapable of disposing, 75-77; fictitious, 86, 87; under a mistake, 88; incorrectly transmitted, 89; compensation for damage resulting from voidable declaration, 91; duration of right of avoidance, 90, 93; procured by fraud or duress, 92; *inter presentes,* 94; *inter absentes,* 95; made to a person capable of indisposing, 96; notification by public notice, 97; interpretation, 98; by or to agent, 103-105; avoidance or ratification by, 116; when validity of juristic act depending upon a third party, 117; date, 122; formation of contract, 153; 154; agency, 169; right of choice exercised by, 209; rescission of contract, 258; performance by third person, 269; joint liability, 272; release to one of joint

Index

debtors, 276; time for payment, 316; set-off, 335; release, 343; revocation of gift, 419; prolongation of lease, 451; revocation of superficies, 836; revocation of yung-tien, 847; to become owner of thing, 945.

Deed—see Document.

Default—Of debtor, 229-233, 254; of creditor, 224-241; joint obligation, 278, 289; lodgment, 326; sale by instalment, 389; of lessee, 440; of employer, 487; of principal debtor, 750; of superficiary, 836; of yung-tien-holder, 846.

Defect—see Warranty.

Defence (necessary)—149, 150.

Demand — Interruption of prescription, 129, 130; joint obligation, 285.

Deposit—Definition, 589; general usage, 590, 591; custody of thing, 592-594; entrusted to a third party, 592, 593; expenses, 595; defects of thing deposited; return of thing deposited, 597-600; remuneration, 601; fungible things, 602; money, 603; attachment, 604; prescription, 605; responsibility of proprietor of restaurant or hotel, 606-611; proprietor's right of retention, 612; prescription, 611; provisions applicable to commission agency, 683; applicable to warehousing, 614; find, 804.

Destruction — see Loss, theft, destruction.

Deterioration — see Loss, theft, destruction and Warranty.

Dien—Definition, 911; duration, 912, 913; sub-dien, 915, 916; transfer, 917; rights of dien-maker, 918, 919; lost or destroyed, 920-922; dien-holder may acquire ownership, 926; reimbursement of beneficial expenses, 927.

Directors — Juristic person, 27; liability of juristic person for their acts, 28; disobeying supervising order of authorities, 33; declaring bankruptcy of juristic person, 35; power of liquidation, 37; associations, 47, 48, 50, 51; foundations, 61, 63, 64; also see Good administrator.

Disappearance—8, 10.

Discernment — absence of, 75; committing wrongful act during, 187.

Disposing capacity—see Capacity.

Disposition of property—118.

Dissolution—Juristic person, 36, 37, 44; association, 57, 58; foundation, 65; partnership, 692; sleeping partnership, 708.

Dividends — Prescription, 126; partnership, 804; pledge, 910.

Divisible (obligation or prestation)—271, 318, 524; see also Indivisible.

Document—Written power of agency, 109; disposition without title, 118; deed of transfer, 297; surrender of document embodying obligation, 308, 325; bill of

Index

lading, 630; instrument, 723; partition of joint property, 826.

Domicile — Definition of, 20; natural persons, 21, 22, 23, 24; juristic person, 29, 44; association, 48; foundation, 61; performance at place of creditor's domicile, 314, 317; surety, change of debtor's domicile, 746, 750.

Donation—see Gift, Endowment.

Druggists—P r e s c r i p t i o n of charges, 127.

Duress—92, 93, 105.

E

Earnest money—248.

Effects of obligations—Performed in honesty and good faith, 219; responsibility for negligence, 220, 222-224; without disposing capacity, 221; performance impossible, 225, 226; compulsory execution, 227; transfer of claims after compensation, 228; default of debtor, 229-233; default of creditor, 234-241; exercise of rights of debtor, 242, 243; cancellation of acts prejudicial to rights of creditor, 244, 245.

Employee—Responsibility of juristic person for wrongful act of, 28; responsibility of employer, 188, 224; see also Hire of work.

Employer—Wrongful acts of employer, 188; responsibility for agent, 224; see Hire of work.

Endorsement—Godown warrant, 618; bill of lading, 628; transfer of order of payment, 716; · pledge, instrument to bearer, 908, 909.

Endowment—Act of, 60.

Enrichment—Undue, see Undue enrichment.

Error—see Mistake, Fault.

Estimate—506.

Exchange—398, 399.

Execution (proceedings in)—Interruption of prescription, 129, 136; compulsory, 745, 759.

Exercise of rights—148-152.

Expenses (necessary or beneficial) —176, 240, 259, 375, 382, 431, 456, 461, 546, 582, 595, 678, 927, 934, 955, 957.

Expert—Remuneration for technical, 127.

Expressions—4.

Expropriation—759.

Extinction of obligations—By prescription, 144; of joint obligation, 274, 286; securities and accessories, 307; return or cancellation of document, 308; performance, 309-324; presumed, 325; lodgment, 326-333; set-off, 334-342; release, 343; merger, 344.

Extinctive prescription—see Prescription.

279

Index

F

Fault—35, 97, 107, 174, 184, 186, 187, 189, 217, 220, 224, 237, 247, 282, 309, 487, 489, 509, 512, 527, 606, 608, 634, 654, 658, 661.

Feeblemindedness — 14; mental disorder, 187; see also Discernment, Capacity.

Fiction—Juristic act, 87; validity, 112.

Figures—4.

Finger-print—3.

Fire of thing leased—434.

Firm — Manager, 553-557; commercial agent, 558-564; broker, 575.

Flotsam—810.

Force majeure — Interruption of prescription, 129; fault of debtor, 231; contractor, 508; publication, 525, 526; hotel proprietor, 606; carriage of goods, 634, 645; passenger, 654; superficies, 837; yungtien, 844; pledge, 891; dien, 920, 921.

Form—Jurictic act in legal, 73; contract, 166; gift, 408; lease, 422; mandate, 531; life interest, 730; transfer or creation of real right, 760; pledge, 904.

Former (prior) condition restored —Void juristic act, 113; to injured party, 213-215; rescission of contract, 259; lease, 431; loan for use, 469; source of water or well cut, reduced or polluted, 782; superficies, 839; depreciation of mortgage, 872.

Forwarding agent — Definition, 660; liability for loss, injury or delay, 661; as a carrier, 663, 664; prescription for claims for loss, injury or delay, 666.

Foundation—Authorization, 59; act of endowment, 60; registration, 61; organization, 62, 63; modification, 65.

Fraud—83, 92, 93, 105.

Fraudulent means—83, 648.

Fruits—Natural fruits, definition, 69; acquisition, 70; return, 239, 328; restoration to former condition, 259; lease, 421, 423, 426, 436, 438, 439, 441, 451, 457; mandatory, 541; depositary, 599; ownership continued after separation, 766; falling on neighbouring land, 798; co-ownership, 818; mortgage, 889, 890; right of retention, 935; *bonâ fide* possessor, 952, 954; *mala fide* possessor, 958.

Fungible things—Loan for consumption, 474, 475; deposit, 602; order of payment, 710.

G

General meetings—dissolution of juristic person by special resolution of, 37, 44; of association, 47, 50-53, 56, 57.

Gift—Definition, 406; conditions, 407; revocation, 408, 416, 417, 419, 420; execution, 409, 414; performance, 412, 418; responsibility of donor, 410, 411, 414;

Index

subject to a charge, 412-414, extinction, 415; donor refuse performance, 418; by mandate, 534; see also Endowment, Foundation.

Godown warrant—Warehousing, 615-618, 620, 621.

Good administrator—Lessee as, 432; borrower, 468; non-gratuitous mandate, 535; depositary, 590; pledge of movables, 888; right of retention, 933.

Good morals—2, 17, 36, 72, 184, 930.

Gratuitous act—193; prejudicial to creditor, 244, 245; gift, 406; loan for use, 464; loan for consumption, 476; mandate, 544.

H

Heirs (assignees)—138, 140; extinction of mandate, 557; partnership, 687.

Hire of services—Definition, 482; remuneration, 483, 486; employer cannot transfer his right of services, 484; warrants special skill, 485; employer in default in accepting services, 487; expiration of contract, 488; termination of contract, 489.

Hire of work—Definition, 490, remuneration, 491, 505, 506; obligation of contractor, 492; defect in work, 492-501; delay, 502-504; failure of employer, 507; risks, 508-510; responsibility of employer when at fault,

509, 510; termination of contract, 511; personal skill of contractor an essential factor, 512; right of mortgage, 513; prescription, 127, 514; responsibility of employer for wrongful acts by contractor, 189.

Hotels (lodgings, inns) — Prescription of charges, 127; responsibility of proprietor, 606-611; proprietor's right of retaining luggage, 612.

House—Lease of, 424, 440, 443.

Honesty and good faith — in executing obligations, 219, 264, 571.

I

Immovables — Definition, 66; accessories, 68; abandoned upon fault of creditor, 241; lease, 422, 443, 445-448, 450, 457; works and structures, 494, 499-501, 506, 513; mandate, 534; manager, 554; see also Co-ownership, Dien, Mortgage, Ownership, Possession, Registration, Rights over things, Servitudes, Superficies, Yungtien.

Impossibility — Functioning of association, 58; carrying out object of foundation, 65; prestation, 211, 246, 247, 266, 267; performance, 225, 226, 255, 282; restoration, 259, 262; to identify creditor, 326; redemption, 383; lease, 441; rectification, 494; publication, 527; delivery of

Index

goods, 650; object of partnership, 692; notification, 173, 241, 327, 650, 936.

Incapables—see Disposing capacity, Interdiction.

Indivisible (obligation or prestation)—271, 292, 293, 318.

Infant—see Child.

Injury—see Damage.

Injured party — Performance of obligation, 214; responsibility of, 217.

Insolvency, 567, 931; see also Solvency.

Instalment—Sale by, 389, 390.

Insufficient prestation—320, 321, 322.

Insurance—By commission agent, 583; of goods stored, 616.

Interdiction—14, 15, 687, 708, 743; see also Disposing capacity.

Interests—Legal fruits, 69; prescription, 126, 145; legal rate, 203, 233; agreed rate, 204, 205, 206, 233; in default, 233, 861, 867; restoration to prior condition, 213; transfer of capital, 295; presumed payment, 325; lodgment, 328; redemption, 379; current account, 404; loan for consumption, 476, 477; mandate, 542, 546; commission agent, 582; surety, 740; mortgage, 861; pledge, 887, 890; coupons, 910.

Interest liable — 176, 213, 233, 259, 281, 542, 546, 582.

Interest not liable—238, 239, 328, 409.

Interest, life—729, 735.

Interpretation—Declaration of intention, 89; disagreement of sums expressed in characters and figures, 4, 5.

J

Jewellery — Deposited with proprietor of restaurant or bathhouse, 608; carrier, 639.

Joining—Acquisition of ownership, 811, 812; co-ownership, 812.

Joint—Liability presumed, 272; its effects, 273, 279; debtors, 280-282; claim, 283; its effects, 284-290; creditors, 291; indivisible prestation, 292, 293.

Jointly liable—Juristic person with its directors or employees, 28; participants of wrongful acts, 185; person without disposing capacity with statutory agent for wrongful acts, 187; employer with employee, 188; employer with contractor, 189; assumption of debt, 305, 306; loan for use, borrowers, 471; carriage, transported by several successive carriers, 637; partners for deficit, 681; sureties, 748.

Judgment—Joint obligation, 275, 287; compromise, 738; suretyship, 750; registration of real rights, 759.

Judicial attachment—294, 338.

Juristic person—see Person.

Index

L

Land—see Agricultural land.

Lease—Definition, 421; in writing, 422; delivery and maintenance, 423, 428; defects of thing leased, 424; transfer of ownership of the thing leased, 425; charges and taxes on thing leased, 427; repairs, 419, 430, 437; beneficial expenses, 431; preservation of thing leased, 432; loss or damage, 433, 435, 436; fire, 434; use of thing leased, 483; payment of rent, 439-442; prescription in rent, 126; sub-letting, 443, 444; right of retention, 445-448; duration of, 449, 450; termination of, 450, 452-454; return of thing leased, 455; agricultural land, 457-463; by mandate, 534; yung-tien-holder, 845; dien-holder, 915, 916.

Legacy—735.

Liberty — 17; constrained, 151, 152.

Limited companies—41,45, 562.

Liquidation—Juristic person, 37-43; partnership, 694-696.

Livestock (cattle)—Lease of, 462, 463; pasture, 790; yungtien, 842.

Loan of money—474, 475, 480, 481.

Loan for consumption—Definition and effects, 474, 475; defective thing, 476; interest or remuneration, 476, 477; return

of thing loaned, 478-480; commercial agent, 558; deposit of fungible things, 602.

Loan for use—Definition and effects, 464-465; responsibility for defect in thing loaned, 466; usage, 467-469; return of thing loaned, 470; joint borrowing, 471; termination, 472; prescription, 473.

Local autonomous institutions—44, 803-807.

Lodgings—see Hotels.

Lodgment — Conditions, 326; place of, 327; risk, 328; right of creditor, 329, 330; prescription, 330; object of prestation, 331-333; joint obligation, 274, 286; of price in sale, 368; commission, 585, 586; freight, 647, 652, 656; pledge matures, 905, 907.

Loss, theft, destruction, deterioration—Necessary constraint, 151; wrongful acts, 191, 196; restoration of prior condition, 259, 262; lodgment, 328; lease, 432-435, 462; loan, 468, 472; works, 508, 509; publication, 525, 526; deposit, 606-610; carriage, 634-639, 645, 648, 649, 657-659; forwarding agency, 661, 666; order of payment, 718; order to bearer, 720, 721, 724-728; find, 803-807; treasure-trove, 808, 809; flotsam, 810, superficies, 841; mortgage, 881; pledge, 899; dien, 920-922; booty and restoration, 949-951.

Index

Luggage—Transport of, 655; delivery of, 656; responsibility of carrier, 657-659.

M

Maintenance (obligation)—Prescription, 126; management of affairs, 174; injury from wrongful act, 192; revocation of gift, 416, 418.

Majority (age)—12.

Majority (votes)—Association, 52, 53, 57; partnership, 673, 674, 688, 691, 694, 695; co-ownership, 820.

Management of affairs—Responsibility of manager, 172-175; without mandate, 172-178; with mandate, 540-542; rights of manager, 176, 177; ratification, 178; outlay incurred by seller, 575; *mala fide* possessor, 957; see also Mandate.

Manager — Definition, 563; authority, 553-557; several managers, 556; prohibited transactions, 562, 563; termination of authority, 564.

Mandate—Definition, 528; acceptance of, 530; manner of conferring, 531-534; instructions, 535, 536; commissioning third person, 537-539; rendering account, 540; duties of mandatory, 541, 542, 544; duties of principal, 543, 545, 546; remuneration, 547, 548; termination, 549-552; c o m m e r c i a l agents, 558-564; surety, 750, 756; see also Commercial agents, Directors.

Manufacturer — Claims extinguished by prescription, 127.

Marriage—Minor acquiring disposing capacity by, 13; prescription of claims of spouse, 143; matrimonial brokerage, 573.

Master—see Employer.

Medical practitioners — Prescription of fees, 127.

Mental disorder—187; see also Discernment, Disposing capacity.

Merchants—Prescription of price of goods, 127.

Merger—Conditions, 344; joint obligation, 274, 286; right of ownership, 762, 763.

Minor—Disposing capacity of, 13; see also Disposing capacity.

Missing person—8, 10.

Mistake—Declaration of intention, 88, 90, 91, 105; compromise, 738; surety, 743.

Mixing (joining) of movables in ownership—812, 813.

Money—C o m p e n s a t i o n for wrongful act, 193-195; prestation not in money, 199; restoration of prior condition, 213, 215, 259; object of obligation in default, 233; payment of penalty, 250, 253; rent, 421; repayment, 474, 475, 480, 481; deposit, 603; order of payment, 710; life interest, 729; partition of joint property, 824; object of pledge, 906, 907; *bonâ fide* possessor of, 951; see also Currency.

Moral obligation—Undue enrichment, 180; gift, 408, 409.

Mortgage—Definition, 860; extension, 861-864; rank, 865, 874; creation of real right on immovable, 866; transfer of immovable, 867; immovable partitioned, 867, 869; non-transferable, 870; depreciation of immovable, 871, 872; sale at maturity of obligation, 873, 878; distribution of proceeds, 874; either land or building mortgaged, 876, 877; prescription, 145, 880; superficies, yungtien and dien, all objects of, 882; statutory, 883; claim of contractor on immovables, 513.

Movables—Definition, 67; see also Right of retention, Pledge of movables, Ownership of movables.

N

Name—Protection of, 19.

Natural person—see Person.

Negligence—Gross, 175, 218, 222, 237, 355, 410, 544, 648, 922; see also Fault.

Negotiable instrument—401, 558, 908, 909.

Non-transferable—195, 294, 484, 543, 683, 734, 853, 870; see also Transfer.

Notary—Prescription of remuneration, 127; sale of perishable thing, 358.

Nurses—Prescription of fees, 127.

Null and void—Waiving of disposing capacity, 16; of liberty, 17; resolution of general meeting, 56; acts of directors of foundation, 64; juristic person, 71-73, 111, 114; unilateral act of person without disposing capacity, 78; fictitious declaration of intention, 86, 87, 105; intentional acts or gross negligence released in advance, 222; set-off subject to a condition, 335; concealed defect, 366; matrimonial brokerage, 573; notice limiting proprietor's liability, 609; statement limiting carrier's liability, 649, 659; compromise, 738; agreement to pass property to mortgage, 873; agreement to pass property to pledge, 893; reservation in regard to continuance of pledge, 897; see also Cancellation.

O

Obligation—Object of, 199-218; effects of, 219-270; transfer of, 294-306; extinction of 307-344; new, 320.

Obligation to bearer—Definition, 719; duty of maker, 720, 721;

Index

maker's defences against bearer, 722; surrender the instrument, 723; reissue, 724; lost, stolen or destroyed, declared invalid by public summons, 725; stoppage of payment, 726; coupons, 727; payable at sight, 728; object of pledge, 909, 910; *bonâ fide* possessor, 951.

Offer in contract—154-163.

Offer of performance—234-236.

Offer of reward by public notice —164, 165.

Officials, committing breach of duty—186.

Order for payment—Interruption by prescription, 129, 132; equivalent to notice, 229.

Order of payment—Definition, 710; obligation of drawee, 711, 713; effect of order of payment being made, 712; drawee refusing acceptance, 714, revocation, 715; transfer of order, 716; prescription, 717; declared invalid by public summons, 718.

Order to bearer—see Obligation to bearer.

Ownership—of accessories, 68; transfer of ownership on sale, 348; lease continues after transfer, 425; godown warrant and transfer of ownership, 618; delivery of bill of lading as transfer of ownership, 629; extinguished by merger, 762; on movable joining immovable, 811-816; rights, 765; extended to component parts and natural fruits, 766-767; acquisitive prescription, 768-772; see also Ownership-in-common, Ownership of immovables, Ownership of movables.

Ownership-in-common — Definition, 827; effects, 828; non-partition, 829; extinction and partition, 830; partnership as, 668; of one building, 799, 800; possession of a thing in common, 905; see also Co-ownership.

Ownership of immovables — Transfer or creation in writing, 760; acquisitive prescription, 769-772; extension, 773; not cause injury to adjacent land, 774, 794, 797; flowing and use of water, 775-785; wires and pipes laid through land, 786; right of passage, 787; nuisances, 793; fruits, 798; construction for common use, 799-800; superficies, 833; yungtien, 850; dien, 914; see also Ownership.

Ownership of movables—Definition, 67; transfer, 761; acquisitive prescription, 768, 771; possession, 801, 802; find, 803-807; treasure-trove, 808-809; joining to immovable, 811-814; extinction of right by union, 815, 816, see also Ownership.

P

Packing—372, 635.

Index

Partition—Partnership, 682, 699; co-ownership, 823-826; ownership-in-common, 829-830; contract for non-partition, 823.

Partnership—Definition, 667; contributions, 667-669; change in contract, 670; management, 671-678; partner without right of management, 675; a partner represents other partners, 679-680; partners as joint debtors, 681; partition of assets, 682; transfer of share, 683; creditor claims against a partner, 684, 685; withdrawal of partner, 686, 687; death, 687; bankrupt, 687; exclusive, 687, 688; settlement of accounts on retirement of a partner, 689, 690; new partner, 691; dissolution, 692; prolongation, 693; liquidation, 694, 696; payment of debts, 681, 697; a manager or commercial agent, 562; reimbursing contributions, 698; see also Sleeping partnership.

Passage—787-790.

Pasture—790.

Petitory action—959.

Pledge of movables—Definition, 884; delivery, 885, 886; extension, 887; keeping, 888; fruits, 889, 890; sub-pledge, 891; depreciation, 892; sale at maturity of obligation, 893-895; return of the thing, 896; extinction, 897-899; prescription, 145.

Pledge of rights—Object, 900; provisions of pledge of movables applicable, 901; creation, 902; as claims, made in writing, 903, 904, 908; instrument to bearer as object, 907, 910; prescription, 145.

Police—626, 803-807.

Possession—Definition, 940; indirect, 761, 885, 941; by third person, 942; possessor presumed to have lawful right, 943; of predecessor, 947; *bonâ fide* possessor, 944, 948; of thing stolen or lost, 949-951; fruits, 952, 958; restoration by *bonâ fide* possessor, 953-955; expenses for preservation of thing, 954, 955, 957; defending possession, 960-962; prescription, 963; extinction, 964; in common, 965; quasi-possession, 966; abandon possession, 241; acquisitive prescription, 768-772, 801, 802; mortgage, 860; pledge of movables, 884-886, 898; right of retention, 928, 938.

Possessor—771, 949, 960-963.

Preemption — Superficies, 839; dien, 919.

Prescription, acquisitive — Movable, 768; immovables, 769, 770; interruption, 771; acquisition of rights other than ownership, 772; servitudes, 852.

Prescription, extinctive—Period, 125-127, 147; beginning, 128; interruption, 129-139; completion, 140-143; lapse, 144; effects, 146; extension or reduction, 147; wrongful acts, 197, 198;

Index

joint obligation, 276, 288; lodgment, 330; sale, 357; rescission or reduction in sale contract, 365; revocation of gift, 416, 417; claim for damage in lease, 456; loan for use, 473; works, contractor's claim, 514; manager's prohibited transaction, 563; claims under contract of deposit, 605; claims against hotel proprietor, 611; claims in transportation, 623; forwarding agent, 666; order of payment, 717; surety, claim against principal debtor, 747; claims in pledge and mortgage, 145, 880; depossession, 963.

Prestation—Definition, 199; impossible, 211; indivisible, 293.

Previous notice—Member withdrawing from association, 54; termination of lease, 450, 452, 453; commercial agent, 561; warehousing, 619; creditor's attachment against partner, 685; withdrawal from partnership, 686; surety, 754; superficies, 835; pledge, 894; dien, 925; sale of thing retained, 936.

Price—Sale, 345, 346, 367-372; redemption, 379, 381; reduction, 359, 360, 363-365; sale by instalment, 389; sale by auction, 396, 397; exchange, 399; commission agent, 580, 581; carriage, 622, 625, 645-648, 652, 653, 657; forwarding agent, 664; dien, 911, 915, 919, 923, 924; transfer to

dien-holder, 926; reimbursement for booty or find, 950.

Proceedings—see E x e c u t i o n, Judgment.

Procurator—36.

Public acknowledgment — see Acknowledgment.

Public notice—97; promising reward, 164, 165.

Public summons (proceedings by), 350, 718, 725.

Publication — Definition, 515, rights and duties of author, 516, 517, 520; rights and duties of editor, 518, 519, 521; translation, 522; remuneration of author, 523, 524; work lost, 525; expiration of contract, 527.

Punishment—Director of juristic person, 33; liquidation of juristic person, 43.

Q

Quasi-possession—310, 966.

R

Rate (agreed) of interest, 204, 205, 206, 233; see also Interest.

Rate—Legal, 203, 233.

Ratification—Contract concluded by person without disposing capacity, 79-82; voidable juristic acts, 115, 116; disposition of thing, 118; juristic act by person without authority, 170, 171; management of affairs, 178;

Index

transfer of debt, 301, 302; performance to third person, 310.

Reasonable period (time)—170, 210, 214, 254, 257, 302, 361, 386, 387, 430, 440, 470, 478, 493, 497, 502, 507, 585, 586, 632, 712, 733, 753, 804, 936.

Receipt—309, 324, 325.

Redemption (of sale)—Conditions, 379; period, 380; cost and price, 381; expenses, 382; delivery of thing, 383; dien, 913, 920, 923-925, 927.

Registration—Of juristic person, 30, 31; association, 46, 48; foundation, 59, 61; rights over immovables, 758, 759; peaceful possession, 769, 770; mortgage, 865.

Reimbursement (refund) — 259, 382, 431, 461, 546, 582, 595, 678, 927, 934, 955, 957; see also Compensation.

Release of obligation—343; joint obligation, 276, 288.

Rent—Legal fruits, 69; prescription of rent of movables, 127, 145; rescission of sale by instalment, 390; lease, 421; payment, 439-442; right of retention, 445-448; return of rent paid in advance, 454; reduction, 435, 442, 457, 837, 844; superficies, 835-837, 876; yungtien, 842, 844, 846, 849; dien, 915.

Renunciation—see Waive.

Repairs—Thing leased, 429, 430, 437; on land, 776; by adjacent land, 792; ownership-in-common, 799; co-ownership, 820; dien, 921, 927.

Representation—see Agency.

Rescission of contract—Default, 254; lapse of time for performance, 255; performance impossible, 256; extinction of right, 257, 262; effects, 259-261; termination of contract, 263; sale, 359-365; sale by instalment, 390; sale by auction, 397; lease, 424, 430, 435, 436, 438, 440, 450, 452-454; lease of agricultural land, 458-460; loan for use, 472; hire of services, 484, 485, 488, 489; works, 494-496, 502, 503, 506, 507, 511, 514; mandate, 549; commercial agent, 561; warehousing, 619; carriage, 642; suretyship, 754; superficies, 834-836; yungtien, 845-847; see also Termination, Revocation.

Residence—20, 22, 23, 97, 746, 750; see also Domicile.

Restaurants — Prescription of charges, 127.

Restoration (return)—Thing deposited, 604; transfer of movable, 761; petitory action, 767; find, 805, 807; co-ownership, 821; pledge, 898.

Restraint of liberty—152.

Retention, rights of—Conditions, 928-931; extension, 932; keeping of thing retained, 933; expenses, 934; fruits, 935; sale of thing retained, 936; extinction, 937, 938; statutory retention, 939; prescription, 145; right of

Index

lessor of immovable, 445-448; of luggage by hotel proprietor, 612; of goods by carrier, 647, 653; by forwarding agent, 662; of animal by owner of land, 791.

Retroactive—114, 115, 212, 335.

Revocation—Authorisation granted to juristic person, 34; contract made by person incapable of disposing, 82; authorisation given to person with limited disposing capacity to carry on business, 85; declaration of intention, 95; power of agent, 107-109; offer, 162; acceptance, 163; juristic act by person without authority, 171; declaration of intention, 258; notification of transfer of claim, 298; gift, 408, 412, 416-420; mandate, 549; order to sell, 586; carriage, 642; order of payment, 715; see also Termination, Rescission.

Rights—Exercise of, 148-152.

Rights over things — Creation, 757; registration, 758; disposition, 759; transfer or creation in writing, 760; delivery, 761; extinction by merger, 762; extinction by waiver, 764; lease, 426; mortgage, 866; power of mandatory, 534; authority of manager, 554; creditor waives real right in suretyship, 751; see also Ownership of immovables, Ownership of movables.

Risks (passage of)—328, 354, 373-375, 508, 603.

Roots of bamboos or trees—797.

S

Sale—Definition, 345; price, 346, 519; non-gratuitous contracts, 347; effects of, 348; warranty, 349-360; right of rescission for defect, 361-366; delivery and payment of price, 367-372; prescription, 127; passage of risk on delivery, 373-375; manner of forwarding the object sold, 376; right as object, 377; costs, 378; right of redemption, 379-383; on approval, 374-387; sale by sample, 388; sale by instalments, 389, 390; sale by auction, 391-397.

Lodgment of proceeds of auction sale, 331-333; selling price of publication, 519; to sell immovable by mandatory, 534; by manager, 554; by commission agent, 576-588; transfer of rights over immovables, 760; distribution of proceeds of sale of property among co-owners, 824, 830; sale of works by superficiary, 839; mortgage, 860, 892-894; dien, without right of redemption, 913, 919, 923, 924, 926.

Sample—Sale by, 388; warehouseman allowing samples taken, 620.

Seal—3.

Security (guarantee) — Prescription, 144; author of wrongful

Index

act to furnish security, 193; given for performance, 265; lodgment, 329; sale price, 368; uplift of right of retention for security, 448, 937; for obligation assumed by mandatory, 546; to discharge surety, 750; depreciation of immovable mortgaged, 872.

Securities (things)—Transfer of claims, 295; assumption of debt, 304; extinction, 307; discharging obligations, 322; see also Valuable security.

Servitudes—Definition, 85; acquisitive prescription, 852; nontransfer, 853; exercise of rights, 854, 855; dominant land partitioned, 856; servient land partitioned, 857; provisions concerning superficies applicable, 858; extinction, 859.

Set-off—Conditions, 334, 336, 337; operations of, 335; performed in different places, 336; prescription, 337; obligation not subject to judicial attachment, 338; obligation resulting from wrongful act, 339; obligation has been attached, 340; joint obligation, 274, 277, 286; transfer, 299; claim against debtor, 303; current account, 400; partnership, 682.

Shares—see Valuable security.

Signature—3, 556.

Sleeping partnership—Definition, 700; application of provisions concerning partnership, 701; contributions, 702; liability of sleeping partner, 703; management, 704, 705; inspection of books, 706; profits and losses, 707; termination, 708; return of contributions, 709.

Solvency—352.

Spouse—14, 143.

Status quo ante—782, 839, 872; see also Former conditions.

Statutory agent—see Agency.

Structures—see Construction.

Sub-letting—443, 444; see also Lease.

Subrogation—225, 228, 281, 313, 684, 749, 879.

Succession — Prescription, 140; acquisition of rights over immovables, 759.

Superficies — Definition, 832; effects, 833; period, 834; rent, 835, 837; non-payment of rent, revocation, 836; transfer of rights, 838; extinction, 839-841; prolongation, 840; mortgage, creation of superficies on immovables, 866, 876; as object of mortgage, 882, 883.

Suretyship—Definition, 739; included in, 740, 741; defence against principal debtor, 742; becomes invalid, 743, 744; rights and duties of surety, 745, 746; prescription, 747; joint surety, 748; transfer of claim after creditor satisfied, 749; discharge, 750; released when creditor waives, 751; for a definite

Index

period, 752; for indefinite period, 752, extension of time granted by creditor, 755; result from mandate, 756; recourse of owner against debtor in mortgage, 879.

T

Taxes on lease—427.

Termination — Current account, 403; lease, 424, 430, 435, 436, 438, 440; loan for use, 472; services, 484, 485, 488, 489; work of contractor, 511; mandate, 549: commercial agent, 561; surety, 754; superficies, 836; yungtien, 845-847.

Theft—see Loss, theft, destruction.

Things—66-70.

Title—see Document.

Time—Effects, 102; for performance, 229; impossible prestation, 246; for payment, 316; set-off subject to, 335; see also Condition.

Trade custom—68, 207; trade relations, 929.

Transfer—Claim of creditor, 294; accessories, 295; documents as evidence of claim, 296; effective after notification, 297; exceptions, 298, 299; assumption of debt, 300; effect of assumption of debt, 300-304; assets and liabilities in form of property, 305; amalgamated enterprises, 306; untransferable claim for injury

done, 195; hire of services, 484; claim for management of affairs and consent of mandatory, 543; share in partnership, 683, enterprise of sleeping partnership, 708; order of payment, 714; life interest, 734; servitude, 853; cost of transportation, 378; gift, 407; rights of author, 516, 522; godown warrant and transfer of ownership of goods, 618; delivery of bill of lading and transfer of ownership of goods, 629; rights over immovables, 760; rights over movables, 761; superficies, 838; yungtien, 843, 849; mortgaged immovable, 867, 868; mortgage, 870; dien, 917; property of dien-maker, 919, 920; possession, 946, 948.

Translation (right of)—522.

Transportation—see Carriage.

Treasury (public)—330.

Trespass—796.

U

Unconsciousness—14; absence of discernment, 75.

Undue enrichment — Definition, 179; exceptions, 180; restitution, 181; release, 182; transfer to third person, 183; restoration for counter-prestation, 266; revocation of gift, 419; ownership acquired through joining movable to immovable, 816.

Unfair transaction—74, 252, 572.

Index

V

Valuable security (shares)—Warranted by seller, 350; commission agent, 587; liability of proprietor, 608; carriage, 639; order of payment, 710; pledge, 908-910.

Void—see Null and void, Cancellation.

Vote (right of)—Association, 50, 53, 57; partnership, 673; 695; co-ownership, 820.

W

Waive—Legal c a p a c i t y, 16; liberty, 17; prescription, 147; rights over things, 764; superficies, 834, 835.

Warehousing — Definition, 613; application of provisions of deposit, 614; godown warrant, 615, 616; separate godown warrant, 615, 616; separate godown warrant, 617; transfer of ownership of goods and endorsement, 618; removal of goods and expiration of contract, 619, 621; inspection of goods, 620; goods of perishable nature, 650.

Warranty—Sale, 349, 350, 351; of solvency of debtor, 352; defect, 354-359; contract, 354, 360; rescissation for defect, 361-364; prescription for exercising right of rescission, 365; intentional concealment of defect, 366; sale by sample, 388; gift, 410, 411, 414; lease, 424, 436; loan for use, 466; loan for consumption, 476; hire of services, 485; work, 492-501; publication, 516; deposit, 596; co-owner in partition, 825; pledge,

Water—Flow, 775; disruption of works, 776; draining, 777-779; conducting, 780; source, well or drain, 781, 782; exceeding needs, 783; course, 784; dams, 785.

Waybill—624.

Well—781, 782.

Wife—see Spouse.

Witness—3.

Work—see Hire of work.

Workman—Prescription of claims of those practicing industrial arts, 127; value of workmanship, 814.

Writing—3; gift, 408; lease, 422; mandate, 531; life interest, 730; transfer or creation of real right, 760; pledge, 904.

Wrongful acts—see Acts.

Y

Yungtien—Definition, 842; non-transfer of right, 843, 849; reduction or release of rent, 844; non-payment of rent, revocation, 845, 846, 847, 849; extinction, 848; effects, 850; mortgage, 882, 883.

Printed at the Press of Kelly and Walsh, Ltd., Shanghai.